Getting down to business

A practical, no-nonsense
guide to growing
your small business

DOUG D'AUBREY • MATTHEW CHUCK

Getting Down to Business: A practical, no-nonsense guide to growing your small business

© Doug D'Aubrey and Matthew Chuck

ISBN 978-1-909116-05-4

Published in 2013 by SRA Books

Printed in the UK by TJ International, Padstow

Contents

Foreword

We were like a lot of other small husband-and-wife businesses, I suspect. We had found a niche that was working for us, but in a stop-start, hand-to-mouth sort of way. When we had a contract, everything was OK; when we didn't have a contract, it was panic stations.

All the same, we were trundling along relatively OK, when Wayne, my husband, dislocated his knee and had to spend a substantial length of time out of the business. Now it wasn't just panic stations, it was full-blown panic.

Wayne had come across the Momentum programme a few months before, and we decided it was time to get some expert help if we were to save the business from foundering.

We soon more than exceeded break-even point and we now consistently trade at a level 25 times our starting point.

It's partly a question of getting all the right systems in place. It's partly a question of having someone to hold you accountable – 'Have you done this yet? Why haven't you done that?' Even if you know what you should be doing, you're much more likely to do it if someone you like and respect is chivvying you in the background.

We are more than busy now, and still use all the Momentum principles to this day. I can quite honestly say that the Momentum programme saved our business. I can't recommend it – and this book – highly enough.

Jo Pearce
Managing Director
Eaglet Business Systems Ltd.
June 2013

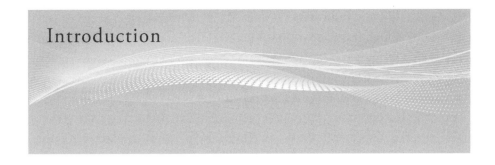

Introduction

We recently met an electrician who told us about his first year in business, working for himself:

> *"Me and my mate worked for this guy, and we did OK, but he was doing really well out of it, so we said to ourselves, why don't we do this ourselves and keep the cash instead of him getting it? In a year we'll be laughing. So we handed in our notice and started doing it ourselves. Well, it's now a year, and we're not laughing. In fact, it's really hard. We never thought it would be so tough."*

This is typical of many experiences we've heard over the years. In fact, the Momentum programme was developed and launched to help people just like this.

Now, ten years on, much has changed. In the UK, there are one million more people with their own business than in 2000, despite the depressing failure rate for start-ups. This transformation in the UK's business scene has occurred for all sorts of reasons, but some things have not changed. The electrician provides a perfect example. Many people start their own business based on their particular skills and interests, but have little or no experience of running a business, which requires knowledge and skills they are unlikely to have needed or acquired.

This book draws together the most important features of running a small business. It is essentially the written version of the Momentum managed growth programme, which has helped dozens of business owners to grow their businesses and realise their ambitions. It is aimed at those who have been running for a while and are now either struggling to keep going or have reached a plateau and are unsure how to move forward and grow further.

The book is divided into five chapters. Each chapter looks at one aspect of running a business. The chapters are divided into sections that go into greater detail. Each section stands alone and can be dipped into at will, although the sections follow each other in a logical sequence. Whether taken alone or together, we are confident that you will find what you want to know about running your own business or where to turn for specialist help. Above all, **the book should help you formulate a plan of action to grow your business**.

As you read through the book, you will almost certainly think of things to do. You may care to make a note of them as soon as you think of them in the Notes section at the end of the book; by the time you have finished, you will have a collection of thoughts that you can then weave into your plan. If you add a page number to each note, you will be able to refer back later to the passage that triggered the thought.

Finally, we know from our own experience that it is one thing to read it in a book or hear someone talk about it and quite another to be able to discuss it with someone who understands and can empathise. We are both very happy to discuss any topic further, by either email or phone. If that idea appeals to you, drop us an email with as much detail as you wish to share. We guarantee to respond promptly and should the exchange develop into something that ought to be shared with a wider community, we will, with your permission, post it on our blog and invite further comment.

We wish you good reading and successful business!

Doug D'Aubrey
doug@exec-tc.com
www.exec-tc.com

Matthew Chuck
matthew@exec-tc.com
www.exec-tc.com

August 2013

Acknowledgements

Many people have contributed directly or indirectly to this book: friends, colleagues, mentors, fellow consultants and advisors, clients and many other people in our network of contacts.

In some cases we have approached specialists on certain topics, who have very generously allowed us to share their knowledge and expertise with you:

HR (Chapter 3)
- Angie Sykes, Rainbow Obsidian, Evesham

IT (Chapter 3)
- Colin Durrant, Colins-IT Ltd, Coventry

Legal Issues (Chapter 3)
- The commercial team from Thursfield Solicitors, Worcester
- Stacey Redman, Client Liaison and Marketing Solicitor, Stallard, March and Edwards, Worcester

Business Finance (Chapter 5)
- Stuart Linnane, Business Development Manager, Clydesdale Bank, Birmingham
- Mark Lindley, Mark Lindley Associates, Ross-on-Wye

We also acknowledge with grateful thanks our editor, Sarah Williams, who kept us to a tight schedule and ensured our writing was direct and consistent, and Sue Richardson and her team at SRA for their encouragement, creativity and production skills that have helped us turn a ten-year old dream into a reality.

About the Authors

Doug D'Aubrey

Before launching his own business, Doug worked at senior level in the manned guarding security sector for Burns International Services, dealing with large manpower issues, training, people management, HR, logistics and sales development. His most notable success was turning them round from an £800,000 flagging annual turnover, to a £5m resounding success story. Capitalising on these skills, Doug then moved into management consulting and training, launching the MOMENTUM programme in 2002 when he recognised the challenges that small businesses faced in trying to access the experience and knowledge of the consultancy sector. This laid the foundation for the formation of Executive Training and Consultancy Ltd, of which Doug is the Managing Director.

Doug is married with two sports-crazy sons, and lives in Dudley, at the heart of the West Midlands conurbation that encompasses Birmingham, the Black Country and Wolverhampton.

Matthew Chuck

Matthew pursued a career in the manufacturing industry at home and abroad, the majority of it with the Chemicals Division of Alcoa (The Aluminum Company of America), where he spent a lengthy period as Sales Director at their Frankfurt HQ, directing sales of €120 million annually. He returned to the UK in 2002 to set up his own consulting business, later joining Doug as a co-director of ETC, bringing with him international clients such as DuPont Sustainable Solutions and The European Council of International Schools, as well as many smaller owner-managed businesses.

Matthew is married with three grown-up children, and lives in the picturesque spa town of Malvern, Worcestershire.

– Chapter 1 –
Setting the Scene

Chapter 1 – Setting the Scene

This opening chapter effectively establishes the framework within which you will work out the detailed activities that make up your business day to day and week to week. By the end of the chapter, you will have clarified in your own mind:

▶ why you are running your own business

▶ what you want it to do for you

▶ how you want your business and your life to look and feel in 3 or 5 years' time

▶ the way business works in general and your business in particular

▶ the key high-level activities you will be doing to achieve your goal, on the way to realising your ambitions

The chapter consists of three sections:

- **Setting your goal**
- **Preparing your own organisation chart**
- **Developing your objectives**

Setting your Goal

"Which road should I take?" asked Alice.
"Where do you want to go?" answered the Cheshire Cat.
"I don't know," said Alice.
"In that case," said the Cheshire Cat, "it doesn't matter which road you take."

This may be one of the shortest sections in the book, but it is also just about the most important!

It is perhaps surprising, but a large majority of the business owners we have worked with over the years did not have a clear goal – or indeed any goal – when they first approached us. Of course, they all wanted to succeed and make money to support their families and lifestyle, but there was no clear vision of where they wanted to take the business or even why they went into business in the first place.

We have found that it is really necessary to articulate a clear goal for the business, and preferably one that is close enough to feel real, yet just far enough away to allow the time to reach it. Then you will have a fighting chance of generating a plan for growth that is both meaningful to you and driving the right actions.

At this point, it is vital to understand the difference between a goal and a target. The goal is the required or desired state of your business or your life at the end of the period; the target is the revenue that the business will have to earn in order to achieve that state. In other words, the goal determines what the target has to be.

An example of this definition would be that the goal is not to earn a million pounds, but to send your children to university and to have the option of retirement at 55. This is now a life statement – something which describes the direction and ambition of your life. There then follows an estimate of what income will be required to achieve it. It may turn out to be a million pounds, but equally it could be half that or double that!

The important thing is that there is now an end point in your mind that is crystal clear and is truly what you want. It drives the target and every action you take to achieve it!

Of course, the goal you identify may be a long way down the road – 5, 10 or even 20 years away. This does nothing to diminish its value, but in such a case it is important to identify intermediate goals – milestones, if you will – that ensure you have a goal that is close enough to be real and keeps you on course. From our experience we have found that 3 years is a good time period, and when that is up, you can identify the goal for the next 3 years and so on.

Here are some examples of goals that our clients have established.

Former executives and senior managers who wanted to develop consultancy businesses:

- By spending approximately 3 days per week on the business, to use my wide business experience to build a consultancy that is generating £50K per annum by year 3, effectively replacing my salary.

- To build a consultancy business that does not rely on the directors doing the delivery themselves and that facilitates a lifestyle that incorporates the house in France. The business will be turning over at least £1 million.

- To grow a training and consultancy company specialising in business improvement, generating a net profit in year 3 of £50K (equivalent to invoiced sales of £75K) based on an established relationship with a handful of core clients and in a state to develop further with the full-time involvement of at least one family member, working less than a 5-day week.

An estate agency:

- To develop the business to operate with a standardised process and procedures that do not require M to be there all the time, while generating £80,000 profit per year.

A mid-size manufacturing company that had been kept afloat by its shareholders:

- To have repaid the shareholders' outstanding loans and accrued interest (approx. £800K), to have doubled the annual turnover from today's £2.5m to £5m and to be generating sufficient net profit after tax that a dividend can be paid in year 4.

A life coach specialising in young people:

- To build a national organisation delivering the core service to the original standards and values, and operating with a system that not only delivers a passive income but is saleable, and gives B the option to retire within 4 years.

A professional speaker and raconteur:

- To develop a business around her speaking and narrative skills that fully employs her creative talents while generating sufficient revenue to sustain her desired lifestyle and enabling her to buy her own home. This equates to gross earnings of around £8,000 per month by the end of year 3.

A start-up recruitment company:

- To become an established and profitable recruitment agency operating with three employees and turning over £1 million.

A light engineering company:

- To be completely debt free, with the new design launched and in the marketplace, importing more products to increase business and turning over £1.25 million.

Preparing your Own Organisation Chart

Many business issues we discuss elsewhere in the book, such as time management, people issues, stress or lack of sales, have their roots in how the business is – or is not – organised.

So before you do anything else, you will almost certainly benefit from thinking about how your business is organised, which in the simplest terms means asking the questions: what tasks have to be done and who has to do them? Many one-man bands answer the second question ("I do") and ignore the first. The first question simply doesn't occur to them and they are mystified when we ask them. In fact, it is vital to understand how business in general is organised to ensure that tasks that are vital for the growth and success of the business are done and not forgotten. This is as important for the one-man band and small business as it is for a big plc.

Big companies have specialists assigned to specific tasks in finance, HR, marketing, sales, production, customer service and so on. If they all understand their functions and perform them properly, all will be well; customers will be satisfied and the company will be successful. But just think of the reverse: if people are not assigned to the vital jobs or they don't understand them or they are not held accountable for doing them properly, things will rapidly fall apart. This is not what you expect from your bank or supermarket!

Now apply the same logic to smaller and smaller companies, with fewer and fewer people; the same vital jobs have to be done, even if they are more straightforward and the people doing them must still understand what has to be done and do it properly. Most of the time this means each person has more than one hat to wear and, if there is just one person in the business, he or she will have to do everything. That can be a huge shock for someone who just wants to be a website designer or a plumber, or who used to have a complete staff at their beck and call!

So let us understand, in a simple, practical way, how business operates and how to divide up the key functions. For larger companies, it is a matter of assigning people; for the smallest business, it's about assigning time and hats – some of which look and fit better than others!

We can visualise a business operating in three blocks of activity: the production and delivery of the product or service; finding customers for it; and the support functions that make it all happen. Immediately, we can see they should be in reverse order: if you are setting up a business, you need some basic organisation first, then you need a way of getting customers and finally you need a way of producing and delivering the product. (Then your admin invoices the customer and collects the money and the cycle starts again.)

Let us consider each block in turn, starting with support functions. These include:

- Finance – bookkeeping, accounting, credit control.

- People management (HR) – everything to do with recruiting and managing employees, co-workers and, equally importantly, those we outsource jobs to.

- Administrative functions – like it or not, administrative functions are the oil that keep the wheels of your business moving! They cover a variety of activities, ranging from daily tasks such as answering the phone, dealing with post and greeting visitors at reception, to occasional but vital paperwork such as company files and legal documentation and, of course, the regular raising of customer invoices and purchase orders.

- IT support and maintenance – in this day and age, IT is the other key lubricant of your business. Even if you don't have customised systems, it is now unimaginable to run a business without email, the internet, spreadsheets, Word documents and so on. This is so important that we dedicate a complete section to it.

Now that we are organised to conduct business, we come to the second block of activity: catching the attention and interest of the people we want to sell to and selling to them. This block consists of three distinct functions:

- Marketing, which generates prospects.

- Sales, which converts them into customers.

- Customer service and client retention (sometimes called account management), which generates repeat business from existing customers. This is a sales activity that requires a different set of skills and activities, so is worth keeping separate to ensure there is proper focus on it.

Finally, there is the delivery of the product or service, which can include production, storage and distribution of a physical product, or the delivery of a service. The functions in this block will vary according to the product or service being sold. For small businesses, the issues here are almost always to do with allocating sufficient time and resources to ensure delivery on time and to the client's expectation.

Actually, there is a fourth activity, that of managing all these functions and planning for the future. We will call this the MD, or executive, function and it completes our organisational diagram.

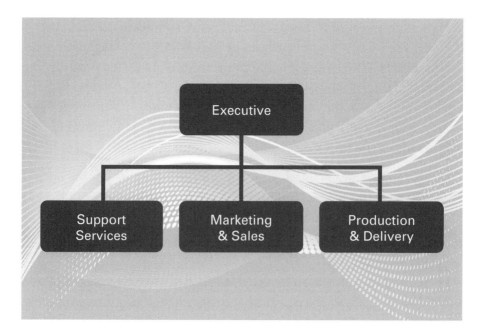

This simple diagram makes it much easier for smaller businesses to identify the critical tasks in their business and assign either a person or their own time to getting them done. Businesses with a handful of people are particularly susceptible to tasks 'falling between the cracks', and this model makes it easier to ensure that all key tasks have a person responsible for getting them done and that each person accepts responsibility for their key tasks. They can now assign the time and acquire the skills they need to do them, which may in turn lead to their outsourcing certain functions to people with the skills and knowledge to do them better and more efficiently.

This simple model makes the functioning of the business very straightforward to understand, to organise and to plan for. It helps to identify areas of strength that need nurturing and areas of weakness that need attention. Above all, it provides an easy framework to ensure focus on all the tasks – and only those tasks – that need to be done to ensure the business achieves its goals.

Finally, it illustrates another vital element of managing growth – balance. Your business is like a three-legged table, each leg representing one of the blocks of activity. If any one of them is neglected or if one grows much faster than the others, the result is obvious!

Developing your Objectives

Once your goal is established and you are clear how your business is organised, it is time to identify the key actions that you need to take to achieve your goal. Even though we have not yet analysed the current business in detail, it will be clear what sort of things are going to dominate the agenda and whether they need to be done immediately or some way down the line.

Let us take the example of a small service business that is currently run from a home office, but is looking to become a multimillion-pound concern, when it will be sold to fund a retirement of travel. Clearly substantial growth is required, which will probably mean a wider market and certainly more sales; it is most unlikely to be generated by one person, so staff will be needed and a suitable office to house them. Investment in IT and working systems will be required, as will the wherewithal to administer it all.

Objectives arising from this scenario could be:

- market the business to its target market and develop new markets

- generate the required increase in sales

- recruit and retain quality staff

- move to suitable office premises

- establish appropriate IT systems

- comply with current and foreseeable regulation

This short list tells us already what needs to happen immediately and what can wait, but it is nowhere near complete, because it is only based on what we wish to do. It makes no mention of how these things will be done and ignores other factors that could affect our ability to do them.

So this is the appropriate time to consider what might hold us back or even threaten to derail us altogether. These factors may be personal, such as lack of confidence, family pressures, reluctance to sell or no cash, or they may be business related, such as competition, a downturn in demand or changes in the law. We probably can't eliminate them, but as long as we are aware of them, we can think of countermeasures to neutralise or counteract those things that could stop us achieving our goal.

If we now factor these things in to our original list of objectives and consider how we are going to achieve each objective, we can come up with a set of specific high-level actions that take into account both the desired end result (an increase in sales) and how to achieve it (establish and implement a sales strategy), for example:

- establish and implement a strategy to market the business to its target market

- research new markets, and establish and implement a strategy to develop them

- establish and implement a sales strategy

- establish and implement a system to identify, recruit and retain high-quality staff

- identify how staff will work together (remotely or office-based) and set up office and/or systems to suit

- establish and implement an appropriate IT system, with appropriate support and maintenance to ensure business efficiency, security and continuity

- establish a system to ensure compliance with all current and foreseeable regulation

Plus:

- acquire marketing and/or selling skills (a specific within the strategy but worth noting separately if they are showstoppers, as they confront the confidence and reluctance issues)

- prepare a business plan as a prelude to acquiring appropriate finance (addressing the cash-flow issue)

If no other objectives spring to mind at this point, don't worry. As you go through the different business elements one by one, other objectives may become obvious and you can add them. Building up a business growth plan is not a smooth journey from beginning to end; you will almost certainly need to double back and adjust, modify or add elements until the whole thing hangs together.

There is one more thing that, in our experience, every business owner overlooks when thinking about threats to their business: illness and injury!

Ignore the cheap jokes about 'elf and safety'; you are no use to anyone if you can't work. Without the security of corporate sick leave or a salary paid no matter what, one of your objectives should be something that reflects staying fit and healthy, and something else that ensures you are aware of the highest risk situations in your business and the measures you need to take to mitigate them. Remember that health and safety does not clock off at 5 p.m. These issues apply 24/7. In other words, in your private life and relaxation time as well as during business hours!

We take this sufficiently seriously that we dedicate a section in Chapter 4 (see pages 164–168) to taking care of yourself.

- Chapter 2 -
Sales and Marketing

Chapter 2 – Sales and Marketing

This chapter covers all the activities necessary to find the customers you need (marketing) and sell your products and services to them (sales). By the end, we believe that even the most reluctant sales person will feel reassured and confident that they can take on the world and succeed!

Marketing, which is the process of finding the people who want to buy your product or service, is a huge and potentially confusing subject. It is easy to get bogged down and spend a lot of time, effort and money without getting the results you want.

We have therefore split it into a number of short sections that follow a logical order and will set you up for selling to people who want to buy.

Sales is the conversion of prospects into paying customers. We have split this into two sections, one for new customers and one for repeat business, the latter looking at various ways to retain your customers once you have won them including, of course, customer service.

We look at ways of tracking and analysing your marketing and sales activities to see what works best for you, so you can focus on making it work even better.

We then look at how to market and sell successfully into the retail market and the public sector. Although the basic marketing and selling principles are the same as for the businesses sector, these sectors operate differently and require different approaches to the marketing and selling processes.

Finally, we discuss product and service development, to ensure what you offer continues to satisfy your target market and keeps that market coming back to you.

The contents of Chapter 2 are:

- **Getting it** – understanding the basics of marketing and marketing psychology. This explains why you need to go through all these steps to sell successfully.
- **Getting ready** – preparing all the printed materials you will need to support you when you get out there and people want to know more about you.
- **Getting out there** – the activities you do to find and meet the people who will be interested in what you have to offer and to promote your products and services to them.
- **Getting connected** – mastering the art of networking to create connections to people whom you can help, and who can help you, to do business.
- **Getting referred** – using your connections to get other people talking about you and referring you to people who will be interested in your products and services.
- **Getting known** – other activities you do to raise your profile and build your credibility in the business community and to become the 'go-to' person in your field.
- **Getting the whole picture** – summarising all these marketing steps into one integrated table.
- **Getting sales** – converting those hot prospects into customers and navigating the most common obstacles along the way.
- **Getting more sales** – generating repeat business from former and current customers through customer service and customer retention.
- **Getting better** – measuring and evaluating the performance of your sales and marketing to provide the data and information you need to improve both.
- **Getting into retail** – understanding the dynamics of retail and the key elements of marketing and selling to consumers.
- **Getting into the public sector** – understanding how to tender successfully for work in the public sector.
- **Getting new products and services** – understanding the role of innovation in keeping your products and services satisfying your target market.

Getting It

Understanding what it takes to get the right people wanting to talk to you.

This section explains why you need to consider everything in this chapter to make your selling activity effective and efficient. A good understanding at this stage will help enormously as your business develops.

First of all, it is really important to understand thoroughly the difference, and linkage, between marketing and sales.

Some years ago, a speaker at a business event happened to mention the phrase 'sales and marketing'. He suddenly stopped, glared at the floor, then up at the audience and thundered:

"Sales and marketing! I've heard so much rubbish about it, there's so much crap written about it, people have written books on it this thick and made fortunes out of it, but I can tell you everything you need to know about it in 10 seconds."

"DO YOU WANT TO HEAR IT?"

Dead silence. A few seconds later, he held up his hand horizontally, with fingers spread out and, counting them off, continued:

"Your customers exist in one of five states. State 1 – they're unaware of you. State 2 – they're aware of you. State 3 – they understand you. State 4 – they're convinced by you. State 5 – they take action and buy from you."

"THE FIRST HALF'S MARKETING THE SECOND HALF'S SALES ARE THERE ANY QUESTIONS?"

Many business owners behave as if marketing and sales are much the same thing. But as the speaker made clear, 'sales and marketing' is a series of outcomes that are linked, but have to happen in the right order to get the end result. Different activities and skills are needed to achieve each outcome, so it is essential to understand the purpose of each outcome and what it takes to make it happen. Failure to do this will doom your business before you start, as you will be spending your precious time and money trying to sell before you know who wants to buy, or missing people who are ready to buy!

We can summarise these points with three statements:

1. Sales and marketing is three words, not one

2. They're in the wrong order

3. Otherwise, they're just fine

What does marketing really mean?

Having accepted that marketing must come first, let us now look at it more closely.

Marketing can mean many things to different people – advertising, logos, websites, networking, social media, PR, directories – the list goes on and on. This can get very confusing, especially when many so-called 'marketing' people actually specialise in one or other branch of it and promote their specialty to the exclusion of everything else.

Before anything else, whatever your business, large or small, you must be clear what you want your marketing to achieve. To do this, we must go back to basics and understand what marketing has to do (and not do). Only then can you choose and focus on the right activities for your business.

First of all, let's revisit what our speaker said and this time put those key phrases in a more reader-friendly format:

1. They are unaware of you

2. They are aware of you

3. They understand you

4. They are convinced by you

5. They take action and buy from you

It is clear immediately that marketing does not deliver customers! It starts from the point where nobody has a clue who you are and what you do; from that crowd it then attracts the attention of those who potentially want and need your product or service; and, finally, it gets them to understand enough about it to want to know more. From the crowd in the marketplace, your marketing should bring those – and only those – who have a serious interest in you. This select band is what we call prospects.

Marketing's job is now done. From this point on, sales takes over. The way sales takes us from level 3 to level 5, i.e. converts prospects into customers, is discussed later in Chapter 2 (see pages 71–82).

Unfortunately, long before you get to that point, you have to catch, and hold, people's attention long enough for them to understand what you're about and whether it's of interest to them. Our experience, and almost certainly yours as well, is that we are subjected to an unrelenting barrage of marketing messages every day and neither of us is going to analyse each one logically and thoroughly before deciding whether we're interested or not. We decide in a second or two whether it's for us and, if not (which our experience tells us will be most of the time), we filter it out so it doesn't clutter our already overloaded brains. We would rather take the small risk of losing an opportunity than take the time and effort to see if it's really worth it. It's not because we're stupid or lazy; it's because our attention is focused on something that is more important to us, more valuable or more interesting!

With that cheerful thought in mind, we can summarise the first two crucial points about marketing:

- **You have to catch, and hold, the attention of people whose attention is somewhere else.**

- **If they don't get it in a heartbeat, you've lost them!**

This, in a nutshell, is what marketing is all about. The next few sections will make sure that you are ready to face the world and that your prospects will 'get it in a heartbeat'.

If it's still unclear, imagine you want to catch a particular type of fish in a large lake. You need to know what bait and hook you need to attract and hold them long enough to reel them in, and you need to prepare them before you set off for the lake. You also need to know whereabouts in the lake the fish are to be found, so you can go to that area; you do not want to be casting your line at one end of the lake if your fish are at the other!

So you now know that you have just a few seconds to catch and hold the attention of the people you want to sell your product or service to. This next phase of your preparation is best explained by means of some pertinent questions:

1. Can you describe your product or service in two sentences, the first to explain what it is, the second to explain how it benefits the people who buy it?

2. Can you describe, in one sentence, the people who will most value your product or service?

3. Do you know what value they place on your product or service?

4. Can you describe, in one sentence, what makes your product or service different from anything else out there?

5. Once you have the attention of these people, what are you going to say to them that will keep them listening?

6. What action do you want them to take?

All these questions are critical; once you can answer them all positively, quickly and easily, your marketing will proceed much more smoothly and your business will grow much more quickly. We will, therefore, look a little more closely at these questions to help find the right answers for you.

Identifying accurately your product or service and your target market

Some time ago, a small IT company specialising in websites asked for our help; they had been in business about six months and were getting nowhere, to the extent that they were within a month of shutting down. When we got them to answer question 1 and then question 2, it became immediately obvious what the problem was: they were trying to sell to the wrong people! They designed software, not websites, yet they were trying to sell to people who wanted a finished website and had no interest in the software! Once we got them to focus on website developers and try again, their business mushroomed, increasing tenfold in a year.

Identifying your USP (unique selling point)

The fourth question is crucial, because this is what marks you out from everyone else and is what your clients will particularly value. We are therefore going to spend some time to ensure you get it right, because this is what you will use to attract the attention of exactly those people who will value your product or service most and therefore enable you to get the most out of your limited marketing budget.

For some businesses this is fairly clear and it is just a matter of articulating it in a short snappy way so their target clients recognise it 'in a heartbeat' and respond to it.

> *One of our former clients spent ten years becoming a specialist in the VAT treatment of the refurbishment and restoration of old buildings (yes, really). In fact, he was regularly educating VAT inspectors on their own rules, which even by HMRC standards were breathtaking in their complexity!*
>
> *His USP was very simple: As a former surveyor and now specialist in this subject, I will save you at least 10% of the cost of your building project.*
>
> *He was not interested in DIY jobs of a few hundred pounds; he was targeting projects of six figures and more, where 10% began to mean something!*

However, many business owners will not find it that easy or straightforward, and will need help in getting it right. There are two ways of going about it and we suggest that you employ both of them.

The first way is simply to ask! Ask your established clients what they particularly value or what particularly attracted them to your product/

service; ask your contacts, fellow professionals, friends, in fact anyone whose credibility and opinion you respect and who will give you an honest answer.

Shortly after we launched our Momentum programme, we were surprised (and delighted) to find that for our clients, it wasn't the promise of achieving a goal or having a helping hand that clinched it for them, it was the guarantee to increase their profits by at least three times the cost of the programme!

They liked the other stuff, of course, but other people offered those sorts of promises; nobody else in our line of business apparently had the nerve or confidence to guarantee a result!

The second way can be very useful, especially if you are relatively new to running a business or need a starting point before you talk to others:

- Take a blank A4 piece of paper and divide it lengthwise into three columns.

- At the top of the left-hand column, write 'Possible selling points'.

- Now fill the column, without stopping to think, evaluate or prioritise. Just write!

- Now turn to the middle column and write at the top 'How important is this to my clients'.

- Fill this column with 1, 2 or 3:

    ▷ 1 means critical: I will not buy from you unless this is in place.

    ▷ 2 means important: It is not a showstopper but I would prefer it to be in place.

    ▷ 3 means nice to have/unimportant: Frankly, I don't care.

- Everything with a 1 against it is an ESP, an essential selling point. There should, at best, be just a handful of these.

- Now turn to the third column and, at the top, write 'How well do I do this compared to my competitors'.

- Think carefully who or what your competitors are. They may not be selling exactly the same product (theirs may simply achieve a similar result) or, especially in some services, the main competitor may be the actual client if they could do it in-house or manage without it.

- Against the 1s in the second column, write +1, 0 or −1:

  ▷ +1 means you do it better

  ▷ 0 means there is no difference

  ▷ −1 means someone does it better than you

- Now go over your list again, checking your answers; take it to a friend or a client and test it; they will probably add to the left-hand column, confirm or change the middle one and even advise on the third. However you do it, get it so it feels as good and as accurate as possible.

The following diagram shows an example of one we worked up with a client, an electrician who wanted to get work with housing maintenance companies and was struggling to pin down exactly what made him unique. Notice how he changed his mind when he thought about each question and especially when he checked his answers with a couple of target clients. He thought the 1-hour call-out would clinch it, but the clients told him it was his reliable, round-the-clock availability that really caught their attention. The exercise also told him to get his story right about pricing and value, which would now be a lot easier with a clear USP.

Why go to these lengths?

Because if you have 1+1, you have found your unique selling point and it's got to be right!

If you have 1+0 or, worse, 1−1, you have a problem! But take heart, because at least you have identified what you must work on, long before you have beaten yourself senseless against the proverbial brick wall!

SELLING POINTS	WHAT CUSTOMERS THINK	ME VERSES COMPETITION
25 years experience	3	
NICEIC accredited	1	0
Reliable	1	~~+1~~ 0
1-hour call out	~~1~~ 2	
24/7 service	1	+1
Up-to-date equipment	2	
Lots of testimonials	2	
High quality	1	0
Price/value	1	-1
Experience with IT systems	3	
Clean and tidy	2	
Great team	3	

If you have lots of 1–0s and you really struggle to differentiate yourself in the critical areas, the 2s may come into play. Some fiercely competitive retail businesses may come into this category, but remember that a 'nice-to-have' can easily be 'done without', so you must find something that puts some clear space between you and the rest of the pack.

Remember:

- **You will now focus on promoting your unique selling point.**
  - ▷ **Get it right and you have the best chance of selling to the people who want to buy.**
  - ▷ **Get it wrong and you will spend a fortune promoting features that don't matter, to people who don't care.**

Holding their attention

You are now at stage 2 – they are aware of you. You now want to build on that awareness and hold their attention long enough for you both to decide whether to take it further. You want to know if this is a serious prospect; they want to know if you can help them. Neither of you can answer that until you know a little more about them and they understand enough about your product or service. With some judicious questions about their interests, and weaving in more of your selling points, you can establish the understanding and credibility that will enable the serious prospect to want a more detailed conversation. You are now at stage 3 and the selling process can take over.

If this is not a serious prospect or they are not interested themselves, the game is not yet over! They may know someone in their network to whom it could be of interest and they could be happy to introduce you. We will return to this situation later in the chapter (see pages 54–63).

Pricing

You should not be discussing pricing at this stage if you can possibly avoid it, and even then, only in general terms such as cost-effectiveness. You really want the benefits of the product or service to be so well understood that when it comes to it, much later, pricing is almost secondary.

However, some people insist on a price idea early on, and it can be a useful indicator of whether this is a serious prospect or not, so you need to be prepared to answer positively without being too precise. In conducting your initial research, which led up to your answers to the first three questions, you will have considered the financial aspect of supplying your products to this market, to the extent that you have a good idea what pricing you need and can expect. Therefore, although the impact of pricing lives firmly in finance (see Chapter 3 pages 114–122), pricing decisions live firmly in marketing (what level should we be aiming for) and sales (how will we achieve the pricing we want). If you have a clear idea of your pricing strategy at this stage, you will be able to direct your questions better and give appropriate answers to people that will keep them listening!

If you have been able to answer the 6-point checklist, you will know enough about your chosen marketplace to know what the market price is for your type of product or service and what value (reflected in a price difference) the market places on yours in particular. If yours is a retail business, market prices are transparent and very public, and finding what marks you out can be very difficult. The market price of specialty products and relationship-based services is nowhere near as transparent or obvious, but is also less sensitive to competition – or rather the competition is more indirect. This is not an exact science by any means and will need continuous attention and revision.

Remember that the job of the purchaser is to try to drive the price down to just above the point that it is no longer worth your while to sell; the job of the seller is to drive it up to just below the level at which it is no longer worth buying. The space in-between is up for negotiation!

It is very useful to know or decide on your lower and upper limits as this makes later negotiation easier. Your lower level can be some margin above your production cost, but more usually it will be the minimum level that you feel reflects the value it brings to your clients. This is more subjective, of course, so you will need to monitor it closely.

The upper level is very often determined by your competition, especially in a crowded marketplace. This is, in effect, 'the market price'. In a less crowded market, or where you have something unusual or even unique, the buyer can only judge based on the benefit it brings them. Is it worth the risk of something new, changing the process or doing things differently when things are running quite well as they are? (This is what we mean when we say that the client can be your competitor.)

Now your USP comes into play! If there is a market price for your product or service, you only have to sell the difference between that and your price, based on the benefit your USP will bring. If there isn't some benchmark level, it is down to the value it brings to the client versus the cost and the risk. Unfortunately, unless you know the client's business really well, this can be very hard to judge and the buyer is hardly likely to tell you! It will probably be a question of trial and error until things settle.

We have spoken about a positive difference between the market price and your price, but you may decide to generate business by selling below the market price. On the face of it, this seems a logical thing to do, since we believe that buyers are always looking for the best price. However, be aware of two things: firstly, the buyer may question your quality or your faith in the value of what you are selling; secondly, if you do make inroads into the market, your competitors are hardly likely to take it lying down and, if they can't sell their USP , they will likely match your price, so your advantage will have been short-lived and you will have done nothing except force the market price down!

One answer to this is to offer a short-term introductory discount to tempt buyers to try your product in order to get a toe-hold in the market. Just be sure that the discount really is short term!

Your marketing budget

The amount you can or should spend on marketing can be very hard to decide and this can be very stressful, so we strongly recommend that you give it serious thought at this stage. If you place it in the context of your business, you can develop a meaningful budget that supports your business goal. Early on, especially, it can be very hard to decide how much you need to spend, when you are not sure what methods will work and how much they will generate in sales.

We can only advise that in the early stages there is some marketing that you simply have to do, and to allow for its cost. It may be helpful to ask other people in a similar line of business what they spend on marketing, but in our experience we have found that successful growing businesses will be spending up to 5% of their total costs on marketing. This is only intended to give some order of magnitude and cannot be taken as a precise number, as it will depend very much on the nature and maturity of the business.

We discuss measuring the effectiveness of your marketing later in this chapter (see pages 87–89), which will identify what methods are most cost-effective. Ultimately, you will want to know that in order to generate £200K of sales (if that is what you need to achieve your goal), you need to spend £12K on marketing, spread over a variety of different but specific methods.

Once you have this information, your marketing budget becomes easier to develop and the spending less stressful!

The next stage

You now know exactly how to describe your products and services, and what makes them special, to catch and hold the attention of the people to whom you want to sell them, and you know what you want them to do as a result.

Now you need to consider what methods you will use to deliver this message and how you are going to direct that message to the right people.

This is the engagement phase, which can operate through the medium of the written word, either in printed matter or online; the spoken word, delivered in person or through personal contact; and through third parties. In fact, all three are mutually supportive and operate in harmony.

However, you are not quite finished with your preparations. Whether you are speaking yourself or educating third parties about your business, you are going to need written or printed material: either business cards, brochures and leaflets that support you day to day, or stand-alone material that people will access in their own time, such as your website and social media profile. These are clearly things that must be in place before you start to engage with the world, so this is where we go next.

Getting Ready

Preparing all the written and printed materials you will need to promote yourself and your products.

Your logo and the importance of branding and design

As you work through each stage of ensuring your marketing is as good as it can be, you will notice how you are continuously building a unique identity that defines and becomes associated with you, your products and your services. The clearest and most effective way of binding all those elements together in the minds of your contacts, prospects and clients is a pictorial image that reflects who you are and what you do, and that the business community associates with you every time they see it.

Consequently, your business card, your website, your online profile, every piece of literature, every presentation, every roll-up banner and even your email signature, should carry that image, exactly the same in colour and design, wherever it appears.

This is your logo. It is the image that defines your brand as you build your profile and become more and more recognisable as time goes on. It is going to be there for the long term, so before you print anything, you need to have a logo that you like and feel proud of.

Even if you are a graphic designer or marketer yourself, we recommend that you get someone else to design your logo. The short-term cost of getting your logo right will be far less than the longer-term costs of a logo that does not achieve your aims, and having an objective third party is an extremely effective way of ensuring that your logo looks good and says what it needs to say.

Day-to-day needs

Your business card

In thinking about the design and message on your card, work on the assumption that the first impression that someone will have of your business will be when they receive your card. A good-quality, well-designed and well-printed card says something about you and your business, even if it is a subconscious message. Like it or not, a card designed on your computer and printed on your office printer looks and feels home-made. It may be cheap, but that is exactly how it comes across. We doubt whether that is the impression you want to give.

Having said that, your business card is a primary means of communication, and the most important information you are communicating at that moment is your name and how people can contact you. Of course your branding must shine through, but it is your name and contact details that must have pride of place.

Some business cards add other features to make them more memorable, such as a photograph, a strapline that reinforces the message or a QR code that contains all your relevant details, for those that have and use the appropriate reader on their smartphones. However you present these extras, please make sure they reinforce the message and do not distract from it.

Many people like to write on someone's card – a note to call tomorrow morning, for example – so please think whether your design makes that easy or not. Excessive dark colours, laminated cards, plastic cards or strange shapes may cause more irritation than they are worth and make you memorable for the wrong reason!

Brochures, leaflets and fliers

Your brochure is another primary means of communication, but this time focusing on your products and services. The same points about the quality and presentation of your business cards apply, but now it is even more important to think carefully about what you want to communicate and, crucially, what action you want the reader to take as a result.

It can be tempting to turn your brochure into a product history and instruction manual. Please don't!

Remember what we said in the previous section, leading up to the six critical questions. In as few words as possible, your brochure should describe what your product or service is, what benefit it brings to the people who use it and what makes it special in a way that will keep the reader interested. You will have to decide whether that takes three sentences or three pages, based on the particular product and target market.

Next, what action do you want the reader to take? Almost certainly it will be contact of some sort, so make that as clear and as easy as possible. Different people prefer different ways of making contact, so list all of them – phone, email, website, social media page and so on.

Stand-alone material

Website

Your online presence can be a highly effective marketing tool, but is also easy to get wrong if not managed very carefully.

The role your website plays depends very much on the nature of your business. At one end of the spectrum is a business with many individual transactions of relatively low value, where each one has a relatively low impact on the customer's business or life. Speed, convenience, ease of purchase, price and a quick – even impulsive – purchasing decision can all characterise these businesses, whether they supply to another business or to consumers. You will therefore need to consider how your website responds to a relevant product search (do you want it to be on the first page of Google?) and also how it reflects those purchasing characteristics.

At the other end of the spectrum is a business with few transactions of high value, where each one has a significant impact on the customer's business or life. These transactions will take longer, will be carefully evaluated with an assessment of value versus risk and benefit and will rely much more heavily on trust and credibility. The website therefore needs to be an attractive and powerful gateway to you and your services; it will give enough information and reassurance to keep the prospect's attention until they decide they need to know more and make contact. On the other hand, they may look at the website after they have been in contact, in which case it now has to reinforce and strengthen the marketing messages they have heard already.

You need to decide where on that spectrum your business lies and therefore how your website looks, feels and is found, but for every business these days, the website is an integral part of the marketing strategy, so your other marketing should be driving people to it as easily and smoothly as possible. It is therefore vital that you include your website address in the contact details on your business cards, brochures, banners and other printed matter, and a link to it from anything you put online.

The other crucial feature of a website is keeping it up to date and the poor message it sends when it is not. Search engines and people alike react well to changing content and, conversely, do not react well when news is out of date, regular features are not updated or pages are left untended and static for a long time.

Testimonials

It is generally better if other people write or say good things about you rather than doing so yourself, for obvious reasons. When you have done a good job for a client, ask them if they would write a short testimonial that you can put on your website and then offer to draft it for them so they do not have to take the time. It need only be two paragraphs: the first says what the client does and, if possible, the names of some well-known companies they deal with; the second says what you did for them and how pleased they were with it. The first paragraph gives context and weight and also advertises the client's business; the second says precisely what you achieved for them.

Online profile

Closely linked to this is your online profile and the use you make of social media sites such as LinkedIn and Facebook. With so many more people using them now as a principal means of communication, there are very few businesses that can afford to ignore them. However, just as the dynamics and language of business meetings and family parties are different, so your business and social presence online will be different too. A useful rule of thumb when doing anything online is not to say anything that you would not say out loud at a business meeting!

Your profile statement is the principal way that people find you and connect with you, so it needs to reflect exactly what you want people you'd like to have in your network to know about you and how to make contact with you.

Email address and signature

Your email address is another way of adding weight and seriousness to your business image. Even if you are a very small business, we believe it is more businesslike, and sends a better message, to have your business name reflected in your email address. Public email systems are fine for social connections, but can send a negative message in a business context.

Everyone who receives an email from you will see your email signature, so in addition to your company branding, contact details, website address and the necessary legal information, include a snappy strapline or news of an upcoming event. However, like much advertising, it's just more wallpaper if it doesn't register with people, so change the message often and make it memorable. (One client used to put a trivia question on his email signature, changing it each week and giving the previous week's answer with the name of a respondent who got it right!)

Signage, posters, banners

Many businesses find good signage and posters effective. Skilled tradespeople, for example, will have their logo, business name, strapline and contact details on their vehicles. Many people exhibit at trade shows or attend other types of meetings where posters and banners can be displayed prominently.

Just as with all other promotional materials, signs, posters and banners need to be carefully designed and produced to give the right message. Whatever form they take and wherever they are displayed, it is worth investing in good quality, both to give a good impression and to ensure they last.

Advertising, directories

Some businesses do very well and generate a lot of leads from advertising, while many others are left completely untouched by it. Just as with your online presence, it is vital to know what your prospects will react to and how they are likely to find you. If you supply services to many customers in a local area, local directories can be very effective; if your business is founded on strong relationships and your clients are spread over a wide area, advertising and directories are much less likely to be effective.

For some businesses, media advertising can be desirable or even essential. Just remember that this type of marketing can take a long time to enter your target audience's consciousness, so be prepared for the long haul and take expert, objective advice on how effective it is likely to be and how much it is likely to cost!

Other written communications

There are many other forms of written communication that help to establish contact and to reinforce marketing that has gone before, such as mailshots, email marketing, blogs, newsletters and articles in journals and the press. We will address them as we come to the appropriate stages of the marketing cycle.

Getting Out There

"My product virtually sells itself when I get in front of the right people – it's getting in front of them that's the problem."

We've lost count how many times we've heard that!

Even assuming that the product or service does indeed sell itself (and we can't take that for granted until there's plenty of evidence for it), the problem of how to get it in front of the right people and at the time they're ready to buy is pretty much universal. This is why corporations spend fortunes keeping their brand names in front of us, sometimes in innovative and entertaining ways. In the 1970s, the Guinness adverts became legendary for their wit and humour, so much so that it was national news when Guinness changed their advertising agency. Nowadays, it's almost a national pastime to decide whether John Lewis, Asda or Morrisons has the best Christmas advert, so we suppose they've done their job since we've just mentioned them. We may wonder whether the sales figures would have been just the same if they hadn't done them, but we have to assume the marketing departments of those worthy enterprises must be able to justify the spend – fortunately for the agencies who make a pile out of them every year!

You have now established your target audience, the product or service you want to supply to them and the things you will say and do to catch their attention and hold it long enough to get their interest. All you have to do now is to find out where they are and the job's done!

Unfortunately, knowing who they are and what they want is one thing; knowing where to find them is quite another. The best fish tend to lurk in the least accessible places!

Fortunately, there are many different ways of finding your ideal clients, which is both good and bad news: it's good because if one way doesn't work, another one will; it's bad because you have to work out the best ways, or more likely the best combination of ways, within your limited budget, and preferably long before you run out of money altogether.

Therefore, like everything else, it will need some intelligent thought to narrow down the choices to give the best results. A scattergun approach will not do!

It is easy to be overwhelmed by the many specialist marketing people who will tell you that their specialty is the one for you! They, after all, have to market their services like everyone else and we can't assume they have identified you as an ideal client; they may simply dangle how effective it is and, if you bite, they've got the result they wanted (or their faceless manager demanded). Who hasn't been contacted out of the blue by a local directory, assuring you that your advert will be distributed to 8,000 local people?

There are a number of ways to approach this subject and cut it down to size; firstly by identifying what to do and secondly how to do it – in that order! You really do not want to waste time learning how to do something if you're not going to do it. Just ask anyone who has tried cold-calling.

We will now describe a way we have found very effective with many different clients. It is a systematic way to put you in control and choose objectively what you do and what you don't do. This is an intelligent use of the resources at your disposal and also comes in very handy when assessing the true value of those invitations to advertise in Yellow Pages or next year's Chamber Diary!

What to do

The very first step is to start with the result we want. Remember this is not, at this stage, customers. It is what we already defined as prospects – people who are seriously interested in your product or service and want to know more.

Now work backwards. What might have caused your prospects to want to know more? Now a whole long list of ideas will come tumbling out – website, referral, networking, LinkedIn, Yellow Pages, cold-calling, telemarketing, business cards, directories, SEO and so on and so on.

Do not evaluate them yet, just let them keep coming!

Let us suppose you now have a list of, say, 12 or 15 different things that could get a prospect interested and wanting to know more. Which of these are more or less likely to be effective in your case? Some will be obvious, some less so, some not at all. Almost certainly, you will say that some of them don't create a prospect in themselves, but they are still necessary to reinforce a message a prospect heard somewhere else.

> *A good friend and client, Mary, ran a bookkeeping business. She got to know and respect a local accountant, Graham, but not much happened until she had a long chat with him and found out what he needed and, in turn, he found out what she was looking for. Soon after that, Mary recommended Graham to two of her clients, one of whom switched their end-of-year accounts to him. A couple of months later, the owner of a start-up business contacted Mary, saying that Graham had recommended her and left her brochure. Having now looked at her website, he wanted to discuss her becoming his bookkeeper.*
>
> *Mary's proactive marketing – getting Graham's trust, recommending him to her own clients and ensuring he knew what she wanted – was supported and reinforced by her brochure, which led the prospect to her website and finally to his making contact.*

A great way to make sense of all this is, literally, to 'get the big picture'! For this, you need to start with a big piece of paper, a pencil and an eraser, and create your own.

In the middle of the paper, draw a circle with the word 'Prospects' in it. On either side of it draw a horizontal line across the paper, so that you now have a top half and bottom half. Arrange the items on your list around the circle, with the obviously proactive ones above the line and the obviously supportive ones below it. If there is doubt, straddle the line, but don't agonise over it.

Now, for every item on your list, ask yourself: Will this cause someone to call me directly or will they do something else first? If they will call directly, draw a line connecting it to the centre circle; if not, draw a line connecting it to what they will do first. You can also use dotted lines or double lines to indicate 'maybe' or 'most likely'.

Marketing Activity List

- Website
- Referral
- Networking
- Clients
- Telemarketing
- Trade shows
- Trade directories
- Articles in journals
- Yellow pages
- Advertising
- Social media
- SEO

- Cold calling
- Strategic partners
- TV & radio
- Local paper
- Classified ads
- Friends
- Public speaking
- Books/DVDs
- Business cards
- Brochures
- PR/Press articles
- Ex-Colleagues

Now a picture begins to emerge, with some key points where lines seem to converge on their way to the centre circle. These points are pivotal in your marketing since they can enable or block the route to your prospects!

All that remains now is to tidy it up (hence the pencil and eraser!). Get rid of the items that have no connecting lines; rearrange the others so they are neat and easy to read and are logically above or below the line.

Below you will see how that unruly list became organised into a functioning, useful diagram. This also serves to suggest many different ways that a small business can market itself and engage with the prospects it needs, although we are sure you will think of some others!

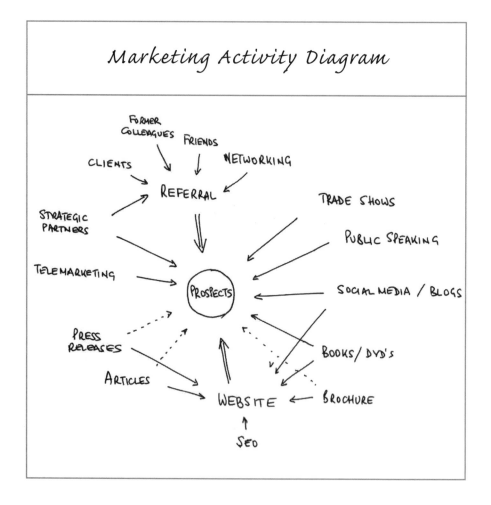

You will almost certainly notice something else: the activities below the line, those that you have termed 'supportive', are exactly those that you identified in the previous section (see pages 36–41). If they are not the same, it is worth reviewing them to see if they still make sense.

In any event, you will now be able to choose the handful of proactive activities that you judge will be most effective in reaching your prospects. You will take a number of things into account here, such as cost, effectiveness, speed, competence, do-it-yourself or outside resource and so on. If you have a marketing budget already in place or at least a sum that you have mentally assigned to marketing, this will be easier. When considering what will work, do talk to other people in a similar line of business to see what they have found effective. Skilled tradespeople operating in a local area may do very well from a local directory, whereas a marketing consultant will use other methods.

Whatever you choose to do, you now need to do it!

How to do it

Having now decided what activities need to be done, you must do your very best to make them work and give them enough time to do so.

This immediately raises the question: do you do them yourself or do you get someone else to do some or all of them? If you are a larger business, you may already have a marketing resource, either on the payroll or outsourced, in which case you will adopt a managing role. If you are a smaller business, where the choice is either that you do it yourself or someone else does it, you are faced with a very individual decision. To help make that decision, ask yourself the following questions:

- What will it take for you to do it yourself?

- Do you need to learn some extra skills and, if so, what will that cost and how long will it take?

- Can the business take that time and cost?

- Even if you can do it effectively, how much time will it take and could that time be used better elsewhere?

- If you outsource, what will it cost, what return do you require, how long is it likely to take and how effective do you think it will be?

The answers to these questions may well cause you to rethink whether you really want to do this activity or find a more cost-effective way to achieve the same result. Don't fret: this is why you're doing it! That email marketing campaign seemed a really good idea, until you found that it had to be repeated every week for 3 months and each enquiry had to be followed up, with no idea how many clients might emerge!

However, remember that it is a rare company that can afford not to keep its pipeline of prospects regularly topped up with new ones, however well it's doing. Many companies, and not just small ones, have suddenly found contracts finishing and nothing to take their place! So if you abandon one form of marketing, make sure you are doing something else to keep the prospects coming.

Just as marketing can take a while to be effective, so it can take a while before the absence of marketing starts to have an effect on an established business. Switching off the engines doesn't cause the plane to drop out of the sky; in fact, at first nothing much changes as its momentum carries it forward, but slowly it will go into an ever-steeper dive, and if the dive isn't corrected in time, the result is only too predictable. It is understandable when a business slashes its marketing if it needs to save a lot of cash quickly, but if it isn't doing things to generate future orders, it will only prolong the agony.

There are a handful of proactive marketing activities that tend to figure in most small businesses' marketing lists and these are worth considering in more detail to highlight their major pros and cons.

Networking and referral

The one marketing activity that emerges from just about all marketing exercises of this sort is business networking and with it the art of generating referrals. These are so important to small businesses these days that we have devoted a section to each of them (see pages 54–63 and 63–66).

In addition, although we have already mentioned online marketing in a supporting role, there is now the ever-increasing opportunity to use it proactively as a networking tool. The advent of so-called social media – primarily Facebook, LinkedIn and Twitter – has made it possible to promote your business and build its profile in ways that were unthinkable just a short time ago. However, the ease of doing this has caused a rush of people all doing the same 'new' thing, so to stand out from the crowd in this fast-changing environment requires even more focus, energy, creativity and imagination than before!

Former colleagues and contacts

We assign a whole section to networking to generate new contacts, but most people have an established business network already, even if they do not recognise it!

Most business owners spent the first part of their working lives in employment, rising through the ranks to middle or senior management positions or becoming otherwise highly skilled and respected in their trade or profession. In doing so, they will have made many contacts and friends in their companies, among suppliers and clients, and in trade or professional associations they belonged to as part of the job.

So here is a ready-made network of people who know and respect you and who will most likely be delighted to help you if they can. They just need to know that you are now a business owner and are looking for contacts!

This can be particularly valuable in the early days of a business, when contacts and knowledge are still fresh. It is probably best to regard business obtained through or with the help of former colleagues and contacts as a bridge to tide you over until your other marketing starts to generate serious prospects. Just remember that business friendships can fade very quickly, so they will need nurturing with regular contact and some reciprocal favours if they are to form part of your longer-term marketing strategy.

Cold-calling and telemarketing

Cold-calling is the generic term for trying to make contact with companies with whom you have had no previous contact. It is generally by phone, although some people will park at the entrance to a trading estate and knock on all the doors, and many home improvement companies will do the same on a housing estate. However, for the majority of business-to-business (B2B) companies, it can be an exercise that combines total futility with maximum misery. There are a few thick-skinned, talented individuals who can and do make it work for them, but otherwise we recommend our clients to find more effective and less soul-destroying ways to generate their prospects or to use the services of people who have turned it into a professional skill – telemarketers!

Successful telemarketers will learn as much as they can about their clients and in particular what sort of prospect they are looking for, what will appeal to them and enough about their USP and credibility to spark some interest in the people they contact. They will then spend time on the phone contacting potential prospects and finding out if there is value in their clients calling them. As they gain experience, they will learn what generates interest and, working closely with their clients, refine their approach accordingly. Telemarketers deliver warm prospects, i.e. companies already at stage 3 and whose decision makers are willing to take your call. This service obviously costs, but then what is it worth to you to have a serious prospect who is willing to take your call? Telemarketing companies charge in a variety of ways, so evaluate the offer very carefully to assess the cost of generating a client this way compared to the amount they are likely to spend with you. Remember, the telemarketer is delivering a prospect, not a client, so factor in your conversion ratio!

Telesales, by the way, is quite different. This tries to take a customer from stage 1 to stage 5 in one phone call! For some reason, it is (or was) a technique beloved by utility companies, who seemed to get enough people switching their gas or electricity on the strength of what a complete stranger told them on the phone. Anyone who has been called at 7.30 at night and subjected to an ear-bashing script will know how annoying it can be, not tempered by any sympathy for the poor wretch doing it. It's cold-calling on steroids, which makes it doubly unattractive, whichever end of the phone you're on.

Trade shows

Trade shows can be a terrific way to find prospects in the same place at the same time, provided of course it's the right sort of trade show! For our purposes, a trade show can be any event where you can display your business at a table, stand or booth. Some are very small, such as the specialised vendors attending a conference; some are enormous affairs aimed at a particular market or interest. Before entertaining the idea of exhibiting, any business will want to be sure it is right for their sort of business and will be attracting the right sort of prospect.

For small businesses, a trade show is the equivalent of setting up their stall in the marketplace. If you are a market trader or a producer of specialty foods, you will be doing exactly that and aiming to sell your goods there and then. If you are a business that operates to a sales process of discussion, sampling, proposal etc., the 'market stall' will deliver interested prospects but no more, and that is why we put it firmly in the marketing section.

You have to be sure the trade show, exhibition or conference is right for you. If the show is bigger than you can afford, consider sharing an exhibition stand with one or more like-minded partners who can all benefit from the exposure.

Once the doors open, you start with the advantage that the visitors want to be there and want to see what's on offer, but remember you are competing for their attention among all the other exhibitors. Even if your prospects are walking by, you still need to catch and hold their attention long enough to determine whether they are interested enough to take it further. This means two things: the design of the stand itself and how you and your staff behave when you're on duty.

Firstly, your stand or booth must be designed in such a way that your message is very easily and quickly transmitted (remember, they must 'get it in a heartbeat'!) and so that you and the people who pass by feel comfortable around it. Eye-catching posters or roll-up banners that deliver the message instantly will be supported by the literature, brochures and promotional materials that you have available. As mentioned in the previous section (see pages 36–41), panel posters and roll-up banners do not cost a great deal and can be used over and over again, so it is worth investing in good design, quality printing and durability.

Secondly, your own behaviour at the stand will influence whether people will stop by and chat, glance and move on or just walk determinedly by. Sitting on a chair behind a table is not a good idea as it presents both a physical and psychological barrier. Standing out in front, looking and feeling relaxed and making eye contact then some small talk with people as they walk by, all contribute to getting a conversation going. In quieter periods, talk with your fellow exhibitors and treat it as an extended networking opportunity.

You must also have a mechanism to capture both the details of an interested person and their agreement to a date and time when you can contact them to follow up. Just collecting a business card isn't enough; you need a way that they will remember you when you call them, and make sure you call within a week or two. Think carefully also before you offer a prize in exchange for a business card in a jar; you may get lots of cards, but are these people really interested in what you're offering or just in the prize?

Search engine optimisation (SEO) and social media

These can be either proactive or supportive marketing, but if your business flourishes either because your website comes near the top of the search rankings or from direct marketing of your products and services through Facebook, Twitter or LinkedIn, you have to assign the same level of time and attention as though you were physically networking. This is where outsourcing may work well for you if you're not really into working online, but just take care that your resource has a healthy proportion of marketing reality (and knowledge) before you entrust such a crucial part of your business to them.

Mailshots, email and text campaigns

These are all ways of blanketing a number – usually a large number – of potential prospects with the same marketing message, hoping that a few will respond. The differences between each one are in the delivery method, the style of writing and the cost per message.

Mailshots have become expensive, given postal and stationery costs and the time needed to generate them, but a pleasant letter is something of a rarity these days, so it may stand out as an exception, especially if carefully targeted to someone who is likely to value what you do. Take care to keep it short and to the point to maximise the chance that the receiver will read it all the way through and to ensure that a PA will not just bin it with all the other junk mail.

Email campaigns are very popular with senders as they can send out thousands for very little cost, using a variety of means as an excuse – sorry, reason – to keep doing them once a week, fortnight or month. They are equally unpopular with receivers, who delete them in their millions. The reason people keep doing them is that just a handful will generate a response and that makes it worthwhile. However, they can be very effective if, for example, advertising a specific event or special offer. The campaign starts, say, 3 weeks beforehand and the message is repeated several times, right up to the last minute, with minor changes each time, for example 'just 7 days to go before...' or 'it's not too late to book for... closes midnight tomorrow night'. Even after the event, it can continue: 'you may have missed...but you can download the presentation notes'. The idea here is that it can take up to ten times to register the message, so it keeps hammering away to ensure you make a conscious decision to accept or ignore it.

Text campaigns are not so common, but their advocates swear by them. They are very fast, very short and, in the right context, very effective. If the context is not right, they can misfire and are simply another nuisance to be deleted at once. If your business responds well to an alert that a receiver can action at once, text marketing may be for you.

Strategic partnerships

Strategic partnerships are probably best observed at work in the retail sector, which we discuss in greater detail on pages 89–96, but there is no reason why B2B should not benefit from them too, if selected and managed carefully.

Strategic partnerships depend on like-minded but non-competing businesses cooperating in marketing each other to the same target market. Clearly, to be successful, they must know and trust each other completely; have similar standards of service, quality and approach to business; and be able to give and take in equal measure.

Summary

Having surveyed a variety of popular methods of marketing your business, it is time to look at networking and referral in more detail.

If the very idea of networking horrifies you or you have tried it and found it did not work for you, we suggest you read the next two sections (see pages 54–63 and 63–66) and try again. Even the least outgoing people can learn how to network effectively and to have fun doing so!

Whatever your approach and attitude to networking, it is really important to understand the power of referral, whether almost incidentally through your family, friends and social circle or through a deliberate strategy to generate referrals proactively.

Getting Connected

Mastering the art of networking to create connections to people who you can help, and who can help you, to do business.

This section is unashamedly about networking and creating your own network!

It is not about hooking up your computers, smartphones and tablets, or anyone else's. It's about hooking up people!

Networking is crucially important to business owners and managers. As noted in the previous section, it is one of the principal ways for small businesses to promote their services to the world at large. Just like marketing itself, successful networking is a continuous process of preparation, engagement and evaluation. It is not a matter of just turning up somewhere and expecting something to happen!

To make networking effective and efficient, there are two different skills we must acquire: firstly, we must plan carefully to ensure our networking effort is directed at the right people and in the right places, and secondly, we have to know how to operate effectively when we are in a networking situation.

We have split the subject into two topics, so we can look clearly at each of these skills.

The first topic explores what successful business networking is (and is not!) and how to make it work for you. We guide you through how to develop a networking strategy for your business that will generate the prospects you need to grow and be successful.

The second topic looks at the technique of networking, from the moment you enter the room to the time you leave, what you do before you get there and what you do after you've left.

Whether you're employed, self-employed or freelance, business networking is a valuable skill that improves with regular practice. More than any other marketing skill, a chapter in a book can give you the key elements, but it is no substitute for the real thing, so if you are new to networking or you simply can't face it or make it work for you, you may benefit from spending time with someone who's 'seen it, done it, been there, worn the T-shirt', so they can show you what to do, how to do it and how to **enjoy yourself**!

What is 'networking'?

First of all, let us be clear what networking is, what it's for and what outcome you should expect.

We've seen several definitions of networking, but in a business context the most helpful way of putting it that we've seen is "the development of contacts that you can assist or who can assist you, by providing referrals to help in growing each other's business".

We should also add a very simple definition of a referral: "a person recommended to someone or for something".

From this we should note three very important features of business networking:

- **Firstly, and to avoid any doubt, it is about generating referrals – for ourselves and for others!**

- Secondly, while social networking is also about establishing a network of contacts, business networking is done with the express intention of developing business – other people's as well as your own – while still observing normal social courtesies.

- Thirdly, it's not called 'networking' for nothing. The purpose of networking is not to get customers directly, but to build a network of contacts that will enable business to happen, primarily through the mutual exchange of referrals.

Essentially, it's about three 'R's: 'rapport', leading to 'relationships', leading to 'referrals'. Business happens most often between people who have come to know and trust each other, and this only happens if they take the trouble and the time to get to know each other and what their interests and requirements are. Getting together for a chat over coffee is a great way to start and can often lead to introductions to other people who may be of interest and value. If such a referral is accompanied by a sincere recommendation, the referral has extra value as there is already some positive expectation on both sides. So while these exchanges are unlikely to lead to an order, at the very least they present an opportunity to learn more about the other person and their business, and the possibility of helping them in some way – possibly another referral now you know better what they're about.

People who network regularly, and actively listen for the chance to give referrals, quickly develop a strong, active network; they get known as givers and attract other like-minded people who bring their network with them. They are the people who make networking effective in generating serious prospects. They not only listen carefully in order to make genuine referrals themselves, but they make sure the referral is expecting to be contacted and they will explain their own business clearly and simply, to make it as easy as possible for other people to provide referrals to them.

We will look more deeply into 'the ideal referral' in the next section (see pages 63–66).

Networking strategy

As mentioned already, networking is just one of many ways to market your business, all of which need to complement each other. Your networking strategy exactly mirrors your marketing strategy, i.e. you plan where and with whom you will network and what you will say to them.

With the opportunity these days to network morning, noon and night, each and every day of the week, you have to be selective, for the sake of efficiency and for your own well-being. It is important to measure, evaluate and refine your networking, like every other marketing approach, to be sure it is delivering the quality and quantity of prospects you need in the time you can afford to assign to it.

When thinking where to network, remember you are creating a network, not a client list. Think not just where your target clients meet, but where other people who know or supply them meet. Get to understand them and what they need, and show how you can help them help their clients; they will appreciate that and want to reciprocate, so make it as easy as you can to help them help you.

Online networking

We cannot talk about networking these days without including online networking, which is our more all-embracing term for the business use of so-called 'social media'. Social media, for our purposes probably LinkedIn, Facebook and Twitter, may seem exotic and far removed from conventional networking, but in fact the same etiquette, rules and strategies apply. So take time to understand it and how it can be harnessed to your advantage. Allocate time to it, follow up invitations to connect, participate in discussions in appropriate groups, think about your profile and update it regularly. And never write anything that you wouldn't be prepared to say out loud at a meeting!

Online networking has two particular advantages that do not apply to conventional networking. Firstly, it can link directly to your website with a click of the mouse, which in this hyperactive world is a real plus; secondly, it provides the opportunity to participate in like-minded groups and discussions, where your participation helps to build your visibility and credibility to the extent that you can become the 'go-to' person in your particular field.

We believe online and conventional networking are complementary, each reinforcing the value and power of the other. Therefore, if you are not into online networking, for whatever reason, it is worth getting help, either to get started or to have someone manage it for you. If you go for the latter, make sure they share your understanding of marketing and work hard to promote your message effectively online.

Networking technique

Now it's time to get into the nuts and bolts of business networking, from the moment you enter the room to the time you leave it, as well as what you do before you get there and after you've left.

"You have 60 seconds to tell us about your business, starting…now!"

Unless you're really good at thinking on your feet, this is the last thing you want to hear at your first networking meeting! So let's assume you're going to hear it anyway and see what we can do to turn it from a terrible nightmare into a fantastic opportunity!

Getting prepared

Preparation for a networking meeting is much like preparing to visit a prospect or a client:

- Are you clear why you're going there and what outcome you want?

- Do you have plenty of business cards and supporting literature with you?

- Does the meeting format include the chance to speak to the room about your business, in which case have you prepared what you are going to say?

- Have you prepared what to say when someone introduces themselves and asks what you do?

- Have you arranged to get there at least half an hour before the meeting starts, to give yourself time to meet people and get settled?

- Do you have your own name badge that can be read from 6 feet away and are you wearing it where people can see it easily? We suggest it should be clipped or pinned as near the shoulder as possible, so it is in people's line of sight when they are looking directly at you. Pinned to a breast pocket, half-way down a tie or, worst of all, at the waist makes it difficult to see at a glance. Ladies should pin theirs where people can read it easily and without embarrassment!

Many meetings will have a delegate list available either beforehand or on arrival. Scan it to see if there is anyone you particularly want to meet and, if so, actively search for them and either introduce yourself or ask someone else to introduce you.

Engaging with the audience

You have arrived, registered and received a welcome pack. What now? For many people, this can be terrifying: entering a roomful of strangers, who all seem to know each other and are engaged in lively conversation.

Do not panic! Most people there will be like you, wanting to meet new people, to strike up a conversation, talk about their business and learn about yours. It's fine simply to go up to someone with outstretched hand, say "Hi, I'm John", to which they are bound to respond. Continue with a few words of small talk – "Is it your first time here? Have you come far? Can I get you a coffee?" – and then be the first to ask what they do. Focus on listening carefully, checking their name if you didn't get it first time and asking a question or two – your turn will come soon enough!

Remember that you are both there to make contacts. If you want to get into a deep conversation, swap cards and agree to call later to arrange to meet up. Agree who is going to call whom and note it on their card. Now you can go your separate ways and meet more people!

Of course, it's easier and more comfortable to talk with people you know, and it's always good to catch up and reinforce the relationship, but again, remember why you are there. Either both move on after a brief chat or, better, invite a stranger into the conversation – they will then get two introductions for the price of one!

Speaking

Now the next crisis: it's your turn to speak for 60 seconds! It's amazing how quickly it passes when you're rambling, or how long it feels when you freeze with everyone looking at you. This is the moment when your preparation really pays off.

It's not often you have the undivided attention of 20 or 50 people, so you really have to make the most of it. Remember why you're there: to deliver a message and to get people to act on it. So do and say something to make your message stick and let people know what you want them to do.

Less is more!

Resist the temptation to put all the goods in the shop window! People are not going to remember it all and the more you say, the more likely they will tune out. So assume they will remember just one thing. What do you want that to be? Focus on that one thing and make it crystal clear. If you struggle here, try this: say who you are, what benefit your clients get from what you do and what you want people in the room to do; then repeat your name (with a strapline, as long as it reinforces the message) and what you want them to do. Since that actually takes only 40 seconds, you can take your time, say it slowly and clearly and pause for effect.

It may feel silly, but it's worth rehearsing this out loud in front of a mirror and timing it! Not only will it be really easy to remember, but you won't be rehearsing it in your head while other people are speaking, which means you can concentrate on who they are, what they say and, crucially, what you may be able to do to help them. It's also good practice to take notes, as that forces you not only to listen, but also to remember what people said and who you want to meet afterwards.

Speak up!

It is really important to be heard. Many people are nervous when they speak in these situations and either gabble so no one can follow or talk to their shoes so no one can hear, especially when they say their own name. If this strikes a chord, try this.

When you stand up, look around the room for a second or two and take a deep breath. Now identify someone at the far end of the room and speak to them. Not only will you naturally speak loudly enough, but you have to look up, so you will project your voice. With just five sentences to say, you will also have plenty of time, so use it to add pauses, show a visual or throw in an extravagant gesture. When you finish, take another second, say 'thank you' and only then sit down. Remember, people want to hear you and to help you if they can, so do all you can to make it as easy as possible for them! If it's outside your comfort zone, practise at home and give it a try. People will respect you all the more!

Afterwards

The meeting has now finished – but you haven't! It's amazing how many people do all the right things in the meeting and then don't follow up afterwards. And yet it's the follow-up that will establish the relationship – the promised call to arrange a coffee or to confirm the referral you offered. If you don't do this within 24–48 hours, they will either forget you or mark you down as someone who doesn't do what they promise. Either way, that's not what you want!

The follow-up is the last link in a long chain. Without it, the chain is worse than useless – not only does it not work, but all the effort and expense that went into creating the other links is wasted.

Where should I network?

As mentioned elsewhere, you can network morning, noon and night, every day of the week. At one end of the spectrum there are events that are little more than social get-togethers; at the other there are intense business development groups that insist on frequent regular contributions between members; in-between there are any number of variations. They all aim to give people the chance to meet each other and establish relationships, with some giving a helping hand with training and coaching to make their events more rewarding.

Clearly, you are going to have to be selective, if only to maintain your well-being and sanity. Your preparation and research will have enabled you to identify your ideal clients and prospects, and you are naturally going to want to go where they are likely to be. Or are you?

Remember that the outcome of successful networking is…a network! It will consist of people and businesses, some of whom you will know very well and some not so well, within which you both give and receive referrals. Your networking is therefore going to concentrate where you will find valuable members of your network as well as potential additions to it. It is not so much about going to where your clients are likely to be, but to where the people who can introduce you are likely to be.

Although this will be your primary aim, also listen to your body! Some of us are morning people who fade as the afternoon progresses; others don't get going till later in the day. Successful networking requires effort, concentration and a hefty dose of confidence, so it's best to operate when you're at your best, if possible.

Summary

Treat every networking meeting as if it were your best client. Prepare for it, participate in it, listen intently, see if you can help someone, be clear about how they can help you and follow up afterwards. Decide beforehand what has to happen for it to be successful for you – say, two really good contacts that you arrange to meet later – and work towards it.

Finally, be alert; before getting out of your car, take a deep breath and prepare to face the world, because the meeting starts as soon as you join someone else crossing the car park!

Getting Referred

This section focuses on the art of generating referrals from the networks that we create and that we belong to, but first, let us remind ourselves of a couple of points from the previous section, specifically concerning referrals:

- Firstly, the definition: "a person recommended to someone or for something".

- Secondly, the purpose of networking: to generate referrals – for ourselves and for others!

- Thirdly, networking is about three 'R's: 'rapport', leading to 'relationships', leading to 'referrals'.

The ideal referral

As mentioned elsewhere, business networking really works well when like-minded people begin to refer people to each other. This is not a chance name, phone number or business card. It is someone who, they believe, can help the other person in a way that will advance their business and they will do all they can to ensure the introduction goes as smoothly as possible. They can only do that if they understand the person's business and some specific way in which the contact they are referring can help them.

To illustrate what a classic 'warm referral' looks like, let us take an example. This may seem complicated, time-consuming and a lot of effort for little return, but before dismissing it, just compare the outcome with the time, effort and expense you put into other forms of marketing!

Alan is a partner in a local accountancy practice. He knows that Brian runs a successful estate agency with a reputation for honest advice and practical assistance. He has just heard Brian say that he has recently entered the buy-to-let market and wants to form an alliance with a suitable maintenance firm. Alan knows a number of such companies, so could refer any or all of them to Brian immediately and let him get on with it. However, knowing Brian as he does and what he might want from such a partnership, he thinks about it and decides that there are only two that could fit the bill, The Coutts Co. and Daniels Ltd., both of which are trusted clients.

Alan's first step is to let Brian know that he wants to introduce them, but wants to check first if there is anything else he should know. At this point, Brian tells him that the potential partner must be able and willing to provide reliable 24/7 cover.

Alan now checks with the two maintenance firms and confirms that Coutts provides round-the-clock cover routinely, while Daniels says it could do it 'if necessary'. Alan decides not to introduce Daniels, so tells Coutts that he wants to make an introduction, briefly explains what it's about and says if they are interested he will arrange for Brian to call. Coutts, not surprisingly, says "Yes, please".

Alan now gives the contact details to Brian, explains what he has discussed with both firms and says that Coutts is expecting his call. Brian acknowledges Alan's efforts and agrees to call immediately. When Brian calls, he is put straight through to Mr Coutts, and as both parties already know a bit about each other from someone they know and respect, their discussion gets off to a flying start.

Brian later drops a short email to Alan to thank him, tell him what happened and suggest they meet for a coffee so he can learn more about Alan's business.

What can we say about the parties in this example?

Alan, who gave the referral:

- already knew enough about Brian's reputation to feel comfortable introducing him to one of his clients

- knew that Brian specifically wanted this sort of introduction

- told Brian he wanted to introduce him to someone and asked what else he needed to know

- talked individually with his two clients to determine their interest and was able at that stage to eliminate Daniels (without raising its hopes or wasting Brian's time)

- established Coutts' interest and (important!) got its agreement to take Brian's call

- gave Brian the gist of both conversations and finished with Coutts' contact details

Brian, who received the referral:

- ensured Alan knew something of his business and specifically what he was currently looking for

- ensured Alan later knew of a critical must-have

- appreciated Alan's efforts and reason for not introducing Daniels

- called Coutts as soon as he could after receiving the referral

- informed Alan that he had made contact and said thank you

- arranged to meet up with Alan to see how he might return the favour

Coutts, who was the object of the referral:

- over time had got Alan's respect, such that Alan thought of him when this opportunity arose
- made sure his PA was expecting Brian to call and to put him straight through without any gate-keeping flannel

Not every referral will go through every step, but the intent has to be there: if you are going to receive serious referrals, people must know what you do for your clients, what you need and that you are worthy of their trust. Likewise, you must be prepared to work the same way in reverse, to get known as someone who gives serious referrals yourself. This may take time from a standing start, but it will be worth it and can reap rewards (in the shape of prospects who are seriously interested in buying) remarkably quickly, especially compared to other forms of marketing.

If you still think it's all too fanciful or unnecessary, be aware that there are businesses who obtain all their clients through this form of marketing. There are even organisations that have taken the concept to a whole new level and will train suitably committed business owners in the technique to make it really effective, combining the use of strategic partnerships with the art of referral.

Getting Known

This covers everything that you do to strengthen your marketing activity by raising your personal profile and with it the profile of your company and its products and services. These activities run in parallel with the other engagement activities to reinforce your credibility.

They are not sales pitches, but a way of bringing your name and brand to the attention of people who may be interested in or curious about what you have to say, especially if it relates to a topical issue. This may prompt them to contact you directly or to mention your name in conversation with their networking contacts, or they may just recognise you in person or in print at some time in the future.

The key here is continuity, stamina and belief, since you need to be in it for the long haul without necessarily seeing a direct benefit in prospects you can put down to it.

Social media, blogs and online groups

These are all online activities that connect you with people who have similar interests or some common bond, such as membership of the same club.

Social media used in a business context has become well established, and while it may not always be used wisely, it does have the power to connect and inform people with an immediacy that was unknown just a few years ago.

Blogs are like an online column, updated regularly and attached to your website. The best tend to be on matters of topical interest and concern, and invite comments from their readers, which can evolve into an online discussion. Clearly if the comment is serious and considered, the participants will develop a mutual respect and become well known in their field, which in turn can develop into a commercial opportunity.

A post-graduate student doing a Ph.D. was studying a contentious and very topical area of family law and began a blog on issues arising regularly in the press. It did not take long to attract the attention of journalists and eminent experts with an interest in the subject, who began adding their own thoughts. It led to the student being invited to become a regular contributor on the subject for a national quality newspaper.

Online groups offer the same opportunity for participation and getting known, and may focus on a specific subject or have something more general in common, such as membership of a Chamber of Commerce. Our experience is that a handful of people tend to generate and lead these discussions, although probably a lot more people follow them without actively contributing. The point is that your name is there in the subject line, so even if they don't read the full comment or article, it has done its job for you!

Newsletters

These are an extension of a blog and have to some extent been superseded, but they are another way of keeping your name in front of your target audience and rely on your relaying something interesting or valuable in every issue. To be effective, you have to build up a following that recognises and enjoys reading what you have to say. Some people, notably business and life coaches, will comment on or explore a question of topical interest; others, like accountants, will give up-to-date news, tips and hints. As with email marketing, you may not read it all or even open the email, but the fact you had to see the subject line to delete means the name was in front of you for a second or two. After a few times, you will start to recognise the name and associate it with its particular product or service.

Articles and books

These are both ways of demonstrating your knowledge and expertise in your chosen field. Articles may be in the local or national press, or they may be in a journal that targets the specialists in your subject and who will relate to it. A book takes much more effort to write and produce, but it has a far greater capacity to demonstrate your knowledge. If it is well written and well produced, it can do wonders for your credibility and standing, and may even become a profitable sideline in its own right!

PR and press releases

These are ways to get something about you or your company into the press, and therefore in front of a wide audience, for nothing. Editors and journalists know this of course, so are very wary of publishing anything that smacks of a sales pitch. However, if it relates to something of public interest, such as generating employment or a prestigious award reflecting well on the area, it is likely to be well received.

Advertising (print, posters)

Finally, there is advertising. It covers a huge range of activities, from putting glossy leaflets through doors, to space in newspapers and directories, to commercials on TV, to billboards on the side of the road. Ultimately, it comes down to one of two things: letting people know you exist or keeping your brand in the public eye.

You need to decide which applies to you. As a small business, it is more likely to be the former. Local tradespeople can do very well from door-to-door leafleting, for example. When creating a leaflet, the same things apply as to creating a brochure (see page 38).

Now you must decide what will be the most effective way to get your message across. Knowing that you have to deliver a message at least seven times before it registers, is the amount you are going to spend on it going to deliver the prospects you want?

Getting the Whole Picture

This is the point where we bring all the elements of the last six sections under one roof. We have identified many different ways to prepare and engage with a target audience. Hopefully you can now select those that best suit your business and your personality and create your own 'whole picture'. This effectively becomes your marketing strategy.

In order to give it life and make things happen, you will now need to establish a detailed action plan for each element, with timelines and responsibilities. It is important to keep to the plan and update it regularly, for example by making it an agenda item in your monthly management meeting.

We are not quite finished with marketing yet. After preparation and engagement comes evaluation, where you assess what is working best for you and how to improve its effectiveness. We suggest that it is better to measure and analyse the effectiveness of your marketing and sales efforts together, so we will return to this step in a later section (see pages 86–88), after we have discussed sales.

Marketing

	In writing or in print	In person or through personal contact	Through third parties
	Explains everything that follows...		
Getting It		Product/Service Target Market USP	
Getting Ready	Branding & Logo Business Cards Brochures Leaflets/Fliers Website Social Media Profile Roll-Up Banners Posters Signage Directory Entries Advertising		Testimonials
Getting Out There	Social Media Mailshots Email Marketing Text Marketing	Former Colleagues & Contacts Networking Public Speaking Trade Shows Cold Calling	Telemarketing Strategic Partners
Getting Connected	Social Media	Networking	Contacts Strategic Partners
Getting Referred	Social Media	Networking	Contacts Customers Strategic Partners
Getting Known	Social Media Blogs Online Groups Newsletters Articles PR & Press Releases Books Advertising(Print/Posters)	Networking Video Clips CD/DVD's Advertising (TV/Radio)	Directories

Getting Sales

"I'm not a salesman" – 90% of business owners

If only we had a pound for every time we've heard this!

For many sales people and organisations, part of the job is not just selling to people who want to buy, but finding such people in the first place! If this applies to you or your organisation, you will need both marketing and sales skills, and for the smallest businesses, this can be both challenging and confusing.

Many people have said to us: "Once I get in front of them, the service sells itself!" If your problem really is getting in front of the people who want your product or service, look again at the sections on pages 42–54, 54–63 and 63–66 and see if there is an idea or suggestion there that will help. Just be sure you are being honest with yourself and that this is where the problem really lies.

For this section, we will assume that you already have prospects. These are the people that your marketing has identified as seriously interested in your products and services. As explained fully in the section on pages 24–36, this is the point where marketing has done its job and the sales activity starts. Now you have to find out whether your product or service will really satisfy them and, if so, close the sale.

Over many years working with businesses that want to know how to increase sales, this seems to be the point where many business owners grind to a halt, and it can happen for several reasons. We have identified four principal reasons, of which, strangely, three are to do with getting prepared and organised, and only one (albeit a very important one) is to do with the interaction with the prospect.

Let's deal with the first three before getting into the sales conversation itself:

1. Assigning time

The owners of small businesses usually have many 'hats' to wear in the business: accounts, admin, delivery, IT, legal, marketing, health and safety and, of course, sales. As we've already seen, sales people in larger organisations often have to generate their own prospects, so they have to wear two hats as well.

If you are wearing multiple hats in your business, sales has to be a key priority for you – first among equals, you might say. If sales is an area that you are not very confident about or you find other things more interesting or enjoyable, it will get pushed back in priority and it is not long before you're spending no time at all on it, other than perhaps answering a chance enquiry.

Sales is an essential element of any business, and this means getting organised and assigning quality time to it. What is the point in spending all that time, effort and money on marketing to generate prospects that you then don't follow up?

> *When Matthew first started out, he tracked his time religiously. He knew that he was spending 60% of his time on sales and marketing, but was frustrated that he was closing very little business. It was only when he finally understood the difference between sales and marketing, that he realised he was spending hardly any time on selling. The realisation that he had to assign specific time to selling (as opposed to marketing or anything else) was a crucial first lesson, as it has been for many of our clients.*

But he wasn't finished: he now had to learn what, in practice, he had to assign time to!

This brings us neatly to the second reason business owners can struggle to sell.

But first, here is lesson 1 again: If you don't allocate time to work actively on generating sales, you will not increase your sales!

2. Lack of a sales process

The next realisation is that sales is not a single step.

"You're interested in my service? Sign here please." Sadly, 'cash with enquiry' does not figure in any terms and conditions we've seen.

Like most business activities, sales is a process – a series of steps that lead from that first expression of interest through to the closed deal.

Think of it like going upstairs. If you had to move from the ground floor to the first floor in one gigantic step, you probably wouldn't make it – ever. By doing it in a series of manageable steps, in sequence, one after the other, it becomes possible. Your sales process is your staircase from the prospect level to the client level!

The exact steps will vary from business to business, so the first thing is to work out the steps in your particular business to take a prospect to close.

Once you have a prospect, what do you do first? It could be to phone them to introduce yourself, if they have been referred to you, or to send them a link to a website for them to complete a questionnaire. Your first step is whatever it is. Whatever it is, write it down. Then decide what comes next. Make an appointment, perhaps. Then what? Have the appointment; then do some research; then write a proposal and so on…

By the time you have finished, you have a step-by-step list of how to manage a prospect and take them to close. So the time you have assigned to selling is, in fact, spent moving each prospect from one step to the next, wherever they are in the process. At any given time, you are only ever selling the next step, which is much easier for you as the seller and much more acceptable for the prospect. Furthermore, by systematically tracking each prospect, you will ensure you don't miss anyone.

In practice, there are two main methods for managing your sales process, both with their advantages and disadvantages.

The first is a big whiteboard on your office wall, set up with the process steps along the top and the prospects down the side, making sure that the last column in your process is reserved for the 'next contact date'. As each step is done, you tick the appropriate row and column to show where you are in the process with each prospect and change the date to when you are going to contact them again, as illustrated on the next page.

The next contact date is what brings the sales board alive! If at all possible, you should get agreement with a prospect for when you will contact them next. This means you can call them without seeming to hassle them because they are expecting you to call (or are not surprised when you do) and the board makes sure you don't forget! Calling them when you say you will also reinforces your credibility as someone who does what they say they are going to do.

The big advantage of the whiteboard is that it behaves like an old-fashioned alarm clock: the next contact date stares out at you without blinking each time you come in the office, whatever else is on your mind at the time, and because it's unlike any other piece of equipment you have, you can't miss it! It is a loud, unmistakeable and unforgiving reminder of the time you must assign to selling!

The second method is a similar table set up on a spreadsheet or, for more sophisticated businesses, in customised CRM software. The advantage here is that, unlike a whiteboard, it maintains a record of your selling and, if set up properly, will generate the sales statistics you need to measure and improve the effectiveness of your sales and marketing. See our example of a sales spreadsheet on page 76. The disadvantage is that if a whiteboard is like an alarm clock, a spreadsheet is like a watch: you have to deliberately look at it first before you get the message!

Lesson 2: Whichever system works for you, establish a sales process and work to it!

PROSPECT	1ST CONTACT	APPT	PROPOSAL	FOLLOW UP	FOLLOW UP	CLOSE	DATE OF NEXT CONTACT	SOURCE OF PROSPECT	NOTES
PETER SMITH	✓	10/5	✓				14/5	CLIENT/R	FBR THINKING
GILL HAMPTON	✓	17/4					3/6	T/S	FBR MONEY ILL
DYE TRANSPORT	✓	27/5	✓			YES!		BNI	CHECKING FUNDS
JD PARKER	✓	6/3	✓				13/5	N/W	
STEVE PARRY	✓	3/4	✓			YES!		N/W	
OWL BOOKSHOP	✓	27/4	✓				13/5	BNI	
PETER GRAHAM	✓	13/4	✓	✓			13/5	CLIENT/R	V INTERESTED
KEVIN BOLSOR	✓	11/4	✓	✓	J/I		14/5	BNI	AWAY
DAVE'S CAFE	✓						20/6	CLIENT R	FBR
SIMON BROWN	✓	11/5	✓	✓			13/5	BNI	NO FUNDS YET
TONY GEORGE	✓	11/4	✓	✓			15/5	CLIENT/R	V INTERESTED?
MD PATEL	✓	1/5	✓			YES!		BNI	
SUE ARNALD	✓	N/4					14/5	BNI	NEED TO TALK R CUSTOM
CLOWN CLEANING	✓	14/5					14/5	SPEAKING	FBR
JEAN KENT	✓	15/5					15/6	SPEAKING	FBR
HALLY DAY	✓	17/5					17/5	SPEAKING	FBR
DYLAN RAYBOLD	✓	22/5					22/5	SPEAKING	FBR
EMMA JONES	✓	18/6					18/6	T/S	FBR
PHIL STEPHENS	✓	11/6					11/6	T/S	FBR
JJ SOCKS	✓	11/6					11/6	T/S	FBR

Example of a sales board

Last Update
01-Aug

Service	Status	Name	Company	Date first contact/referral	Origin	Date first apptmt	follow up	Proposal	Proposal follow up	Date closed	NEXT CONTACT	Summary
C	A	Bruce Campbell	Nova Energy Ltd	10-Jul	Chamber	17-Jul	24-Jul	24-Jul			10-Aug	No news at 29/1 nor 13/3 - review 1/4
C	A	Leslie Hook	Huberts	11-Jul	Chamber	16-Jul	21-Jul				04-Aug	Follow up booked for 28/7, pp to 4/8,
M	A	Jane Black	Black Cat Media	12-Mar	BC Chamber Trade Show	14-May	28-May	28-May	28-Jun		10-Aug	Third follow up - abandon if dont close
C	A	Rosie Green	Belljar Services	14-May	LinkedIn	14-Jun		14-Jun			11-Aug	
C	A	Zaheed Gupta	TRG Accountants	14-Jun	Acctnt Referral	15-Jun	22-Jun	22-Jun	22-Jul		10-Aug	
C	A	C Crompton	J and K Associates	27-Jul	Networking						11-Aug	
C	A	A Douglas	Trenshaws	27-Jul	Networking						11-Aug	
T	B	Bill Downing	ISB	07-Jun	Client Referral						07-Sep	Interested but not yet - talk again September
M	X	Jack Watson	ICSI Management	14-May	Telemarketing	24-May	31-May	31-May	14-Jun	15-Jul	-	CLOSED
M	Z	Dave Hill	Hillside Telecom	12-Mar	BC Chamber Trade Show	15-May					-	2/7 - Hasn't responded to any calls - abandoned

total at 02-Jul
this month

	Live Prospects	All Prospects	New Appts	Proposals/Quotes	Closures
total at	5	5	3	1	1
this month	3	5	4	4	0
Bruce Campbell	1	1	1	1	0
Leslie Hook	1	1	1	0	0
Jane Black	1	1	1	1	0
Rosie Green	1	1	1	1	0
Zaheed Gupta	1	1	1	1	0
C Crompton	1	1	0	0	0
A Douglas	1	1	0	0	0
Bill Downing	1	1	0	0	1
Jack Watson	0	1	1	1	0
Dave Hill	0	1	1	0	0
	0	0	0	0	0
	0	0	0	0	0
	0	0	0	0	0
	0	0	0	0	0

Example of a sales spreadsheet

3. Lack of delivery resource

Even when the time was assigned to follow an established sales process, we still found some business owners were not selling, and the reason was much more common than you might imagine.

If you are responsible for selling and delivery (which many small-business owners are), your brain may be telling you not to close the deal because you're worried you can't deliver it! Can you believe it?! All that hard work and expense to tell the world about your services and find people who want to buy – and then you say no?

Skilled tradespeople are very susceptible to this; we call it the 'no one does it as well as me' syndrome, because this is why they won't work with or train others to help them deal with the volume of work. Consultancies and other highly relationship-based businesses can be similarly afflicted, unless the business owner is very careful to bring in other people at the outset and manage clients' expectations accordingly.

> Even in a larger business, this can happen. Sales at a £5 million turnover security company had dried up; the sales manager talked to his sales force and discovered they were regularly in contact with the scheduling team, who were always complaining they didn't have enough staff to deliver the contracts. So the sales team got the idea they shouldn't sell in case their colleagues couldn't deliver the quality service. By separating the two teams, and getting sales focused on selling and scheduling focused on getting the right staff to deliver, sales increased and customers continued to be satisfied!

In this example, the solution lay in understanding how the problem arose and managing the two departments differently. The owners of smaller businesses will probably not have that room for manoeuvre and will have to ask themselves some searching questions about the original goal for the business. Ultimately, the solution will come down to one of two choices.

Firstly, can your business goal be achieved without adding any more delivery resources? It may not be about extra clients; it may be that if the service or product is in sufficient demand, a higher price will achieve the financial goal without jeopardising the business. It may be a time management issue, in which better use of time could release extra delivery time (time management is discussed more in Chapter 4 pages 148–156).

However, if it becomes clear that the goal cannot be achieved with your current resources and organisation, you will have to add to them. This is where people who are used to working on their own or in a very small unit can really struggle. In our experience, such people are as likely to adjust their goal to match their earning capacity, as they are to accept the distraction, time and trouble of adding and training staff or associates. It also brings into sharp relief whether it's client contact or managing other people that really floats your boat. The earlier you acknowledge which it is, and plan accordingly, the better!

If your original goal was to expand the business with extra staff or associates, and you were sure you wanted to manage other people (whether staff or independent associates or both), your growth plan will have included the task of recruiting, training and retaining suitable candidates in time to have the resources you need available when you require them. You just have to be aware how long it will take to do this and start the process in plenty of time.

Judging the right time is never easy and requires the confidence that you can meet your growth plan, but by using your network judiciously (see pages 54–63) you can become aware of suitable associates or staff in time to make a considered decision, without the pressure of finding someone to deliver the contract that has to start next week!

Finally, remember that the client is the judge of acceptable quality, not you. Contrary to what some of our clients have said, other people can do it just as well as you – it's just a matter of finding them. Perfectionists will always struggle with this!

Lesson 3: It is vital to make sure you have enough delivery resources in place, so that whoever is doing the selling believes the product or service can be delivered as promised to the customer.

4. The sales conversation

There are not many people who really enjoy selling, which is perhaps why so many business owners have told us: "I'm not a salesman". Many of them went into business to earn money from using their particular skill or talent, and to them, selling is a disagreeable distraction that eats into their earning time. Others perceive selling as bullying people into buying things they don't need or want, at prices they can't afford. Or perhaps they just mean that the advantages of their product or service are obvious, so why can't people just buy it and stop wasting everyone's time?

Whatever the reason, these thought processes need replacing with some practical advice on how to talk to a prospect and bring the discussion to a satisfactory conclusion.

First of all, let us remind ourselves what our furious speaker said about sales at the beginning of this chapter (see page 24): Sales takes you from step 3 – your customer understands you, to step 5 – your customer buys from you.

There is a big clue here: there is a step 4 – the customer is convinced by you!

So firstly we must understand what has to happen to move from step 3 to step 4. It will probably be two things: the customer must feel that you understand their circumstances and the issues they think you may be able to help them with; and that your product or service is appropriate to their circumstances and can solve their problem. Both of these will be resolved most quickly by effective questioning on your part, both to understand their situation as thoroughly as possible and to assess what they know about you that excited their interest in the first place.

Then, and only then, should you present a solution from your toolbox that you believe will fit, with a brief and clear explanation as to why you feel it's right for them and, if necessary, why you are the right person or company to deliver it. This must be like the proverbial mini-skirt: short enough to retain attention, long enough to cover the essentials.

This may take some time, but it is essential the customer feels that you have listened and understood, and that you and your product or service, are credible. At this point, you need to check whether you have said enough to convince them or whether they need something else.

Your customer may now be convinced, but remember you're still only at step 4. The conversation to move them to step 5 now finally gets into what so many people think sales is about – the price! This can be as much about how the price is perceived as about what it actually is. If the customer feels disappointed, let down or strung along, it will be a much harder sell, so think carefully how you are going to express it.

Your questioning will have given you some insight into the value of your solution, so you can judge whether your asking price represents good value. If it does, you can frame the price in a way that highlights the value the client would get, so that the price is not a shock but is seen in context. For example, your asking price may be £2,500, which just said cold could feel very off-putting. But if you said: "You have said that solving the problem will save you £20,000, so how does a solution costing £2,500 sound?", the client now hears the solution first, the value second and the price third!

Likewise, if your solution does not offer such value, you will have to think again, either by adjusting the price or finding a less expensive option. Either way, you need to express it in a way that suggests you have the customer's interest at heart and that you are not trying to con them into accepting something that won't work or will end up costing them money. At the same time, there is no point in quoting a price that leaves you out of pocket, just to get the business.

All this sounds very logical and straightforward, so why do so many sales conversations get stuck at step 4, with the customer saying "Thanks, it sounds good, I'll think about it"?

There are several possible reasons, among them:

- You haven't made it clear that you want the business! Having set out your stall and why it will benefit the customer, **ask for the business**!

If the answer is still no, probe what other reasons are holding them back:

- Timing: they are genuinely not ready, perhaps due to cash flow or something else that affects when they can buy. It could just be that they need time to process all the information, check out a few things or make sure that the sums still add up after they've slept on it. Either way, agree a time when you can call and be clear that it is in order to have a decision, and preferably a positive one!

- Ditherer: they can't make a decision, no matter how strong the case is. The only way here is to put a strict time limit on the offer. If they still won't agree, you don't want them as a client anyway – they'll be a nightmare to work with!

- Not competitive, not convinced or has simply decided against, but can't say so: question a little further to see if there is anything you can do, otherwise use the same tactic as for the ditherer.

With experience, your questioning between steps 3 and 4 will either head off or expose these objections much earlier, giving you the chance to adjust if necessary. At worst, you will waste less time and energy!

Having discussed what to say and how to say it, it remains to fold it into your sales process. Almost certainly, the first step will be an appointment. Even if some later conversations are held on the phone, it is really important that the first one is face to face, at the prospect's premises or at a place of their choosing. Remember that most communication is non-verbal, so seeing you in person, showing appropriate respect and courtesy and giving the right signals of confidence and reassurance, all adds to their picture of you as someone who is credible and that they can like and trust. Once that is established, a phone call to follow up a meeting or a proposal will be perfectly acceptable, but don't leave it too long: after each stage of the process, agree a follow-up date and time, confirm it in an email and then stick to it!

Two other points about the sales conversation are worthy of mention.

Firstly, and particularly when a conversation reaches a natural break, mention the other products and services you offer. Too many times, people have found a prospect or client had purchased something elsewhere that they could have supplied and been told "You never told me/I didn't realise you supplied that".

Secondly, and whether you close the deal or not, enquire whether they can refer you to anyone else they know, perhaps suffering the same problem or in a similar industry. This is easy to forget in the euphoria of having closed the deal, and even more likely if you feel deflated and sick when they have just said no, but this is the moment to try to salvage something from the wreckage, especially if they feel bad about saying no!

Afterwards

A wise businessman was once very fond of reminding us: "The sale is not done until the money's in the bank!"

If you permit sales on credit terms or allow stage payments over the length of the contract, you must safeguard yourself against the occasional late payer, rogue trader or client that gets into difficulties. You may decide to take the risk that you will never have a bad debt, but we strongly advise against it. We believe it is essential to check the rating of every client before you commit resources to production and/or delivery, even the most apparently sound of them. There are plenty of companies that specialise in trawling through Companies House records and other sources to rate companies and their directors, and who will chase late payments for you. For the sake of a few thousand pounds a year, it will be worth it, and not just for your peace of mind!

Sales confirmation and invoicing

Once you are satisfied that the sale can go ahead, confirm everything you have agreed, plus your terms and conditions, in writing, immediately. This minimises the chance of any misunderstanding and puts you in a strong position should things go wrong later.

Equally important, it tells your invoicing department exactly what to invoice and when. Many small businesses outsource their financial administration and this is a key link in the communication chain!

Getting More Sales

This area is a continuation of sales, but is often forgotten in the euphoria of having done a deal or agreed a contract. Or perhaps more likely, all your focus is on winning new business from new clients. We have therefore dedicated a separate section to it, to ensure that your sales planning and sales effort truly reflects what should be blindingly obvious: it is much easier and less costly to sell to an existing satisfied client than to win a new one.

So now you have sold something – congratulations! Your product or service is what you're really about, so we have no doubt that you will deliver it satisfactorily and get it invoiced.

But wait a minute. Are you sure about that? How do you know you have delivered it to the customer's satisfaction? This question leads us into the realm of customer service, and more broadly into client retention (sometimes called account management). All of these phrases focus on the things you need to do to have customers coming back for more. After all, shouldn't they be much easier to convince than someone who's never used you before?

So now we have the complete central pillar of your organisation chart:

- Marketing, which delivers prospects

- Sales, which delivers clients

- Client retention, which delivers repeat business!

First of all, let's be sure we know the role that customer service plays in client retention.

Client retention covers everything you do to ensure your clients will buy from you again when they are next in the market for your product or service. It includes the direct contact you have with your clients and the many things you do behind the scenes to understand them and their needs better, as well as keeping in touch with them whether they are buying from you or not. Already you may have noticed a bit of marketing in what is essentially a sales activity, in that you are often giving the same message to a number of clients, even if you're clever enough to make them feel you are talking to them and only them!

Customer service is one of the principal means of ensuring they have a favourable opinion of you and your service, and that you get the earliest hint of any problem or reservation on their part. It is almost completely to do with your direct interactions with them, and is the principal method of building a relationship that enables you to maintain contact and keep your name and service at the forefront of their minds.

Let's deal with customer service first, since this can be a minefield where one false step can blow up in your face and the fallout can quickly send shockwaves through your marketplace.

At the very heart of this lies one simple question: Do you want your customers to have the best possible experience when dealing with you and your company?

Before answering, remember these much quoted lines, written by the American poet Maya Angelou:

> *People will forget what you said,*
> *People will forget what you did,*
> *But they will NEVER forget how you made them feel!*

Perhaps this explains some familiar features of customer behaviour:

- They will relate a bad experience to ten people, but a good experience to only one.

- One bad experience will wipe out the memory of ten good ones.

- They probably won't tell you, they just won't come back.

So what can you do?

It all starts with **attitude**.

How many times have you been put off by a surly receptionist, a bored cashier or shop assistants chatting to each other instead of serving you?

You and your staff must have the right attitude. You, and they, must want your customers to have the best possible experience when dealing with your company, whether it is during the sales process, the delivery process or any after-sales activity. Whether it is a simple transaction or a complex negotiation, clients who look back on it with satisfaction and pleasure are far more likely to return. If you have a positive and welcoming attitude, it is much easier to work out what will satisfy customers and set about doing it.

Attention to detail

It may not seem important, but getting little things right can make a really big difference, things like asking for and remembering people's names, spelling them correctly in emails and letters and remembering details about them and their business before contacting them. These things will not compensate for a major gaffe, although they may help to recover from it, but they certainly help people to remember you!

Communication

Talk to the customer and let them know what is happening, even (in fact especially) if it is bad news. Tell them and keep updating them, even if you have nothing new to add. The biggest gripe people have when delayed at airports is 'not being told anything', and the longer the silence continues, the louder it gets!

Good customer service does not mean you are perfect at your job; it is about how you do your job in relation to the customer. It's not what you do when things are going well; it's how you respond when things go wrong. Many businesses sell on the basis of a deadline that, in reality, is little more than an educated guess: creative design and IT solutions are two that spring immediately to mind! The idea that the creative mind can switch off when under pressure to produce, and call the client to say they can't have it yet, is totally counter-intuitive, yet it's probably the best way to manage an already difficult situation!

The WOW factor

With more and more people providing high-quality products and good service, it is increasingly hard to stand out from the crowd. Doing something out of the ordinary and 'going that extra mile' to make the experience of dealing with you memorable is one way, provided everything else is in place.

This can be a little thing: flowers to say thank you for the business; a birthday card; a little personalised note to say thank you for the service included with the bill. You will get positive talk about you.

> *There is a delightful story illustrating this from a small supermarket in the US. After a pep talk from the manager to all the staff, a young man employed to pack customers' bags thought of putting pleasant little messages on slips of paper in their shopping. He didn't say anything, but prepared them at home and came to work in the morning armed with a bundle of them. After a little while, the staff noticed that some customers were hanging back to pay until they were sure they would be in his line. Business began to creep up as word spread about the witty little messages people found in their shopping when they got home.*

Customer retention

If customer service is about keeping a customer feeling good about you and your service during the sales and delivery periods (and afterwards, if after-sales service is included), customer retention is about maintaining the same feeling during the interval between purchases. Ideally, we want them to place their next order with us without even thinking about it, however long since they last bought the item or service. For this to happen, two things need to be in place: first, they must remember that you supply the item, which means reminding them regularly and keeping your name fresh in their mind; and second, they were so happy with the quality and value of the product and the service that went with it, and it was such a pleasure doing business with you, that to buy anywhere else would be unthinkable. The first half is effectively marketing to them, the second half is customer service. Both are founded on and supported by a strong relationship and it is this that is especially difficult for your competitors to breach.

You will have worked hard to establish that relationship. You will have supplied them well and consistently and put things right quickly whenever they went wrong. You communicated regularly, not just about your product, but about industry information that may interest them, news about other products and services, referrals to others who may help them and so on. You may have introduced them to potential clients and thereby helped them with their marketing.

By building this thinking into your marketing strategy, you will not just expand your business with new clients, but your existing clients will buy more, more often, so that you increase your business in the most timely and cost-effective way possible.

Getting Better

"I know half the money I spend on advertising is wasted, the trouble is I don't know which half." – John Wanamaker, 19th-century US merchant

As with any process that you want to improve, you have to measure the outcome of what you do to find out if it is effective and to assess whether any changes you make generate a better result. This is the case with your sales and marketing effort. In fact, for a small business, where you can spend a fortune on marketing without really knowing what works and what doesn't, we believe it is a critical element in the whole process.

Earlier in this chapter (see pages 73–76), we described the sales board, which you used to record all your prospects and track them through the sales process to completion. By doing that on a spreadsheet, you can generate all the marketing and sales statistics you need to assess the effectiveness of both your marketing and sales activity.

This is gold dust! Marketing rarely delivers instant results, so you must give each marketing activity the time to work. Without good data to tell you which activities generated what number of prospects and how many of those you converted to clients, it will be really difficult to decide how long to give them, which to continue and which to abandon. If something isn't working after 12 months, you should be thinking about it very carefully. In any event, you should be renewing your marketing strategy at least once per year and developing a plan based on that strategy for the next 12 months.

In our own business, we decided after a few trials to exhibit at 12 trade shows in our region per year, at a cost of several thousand pounds in fees and follow-up costs. When we analysed the results of the first full year, we found that there had been plenty of prospects, but very few had become clients. We were faced with a decision: abandon trade shows, go to different ones or try something completely different. The few clients we did get were high quality and we were very happy to have them, but when we looked at some of the prospects that had fallen by the wayside, we realised we had expended a lot of time, money and energy on businesses that had no possibility of becoming clients. We therefore modified our strategy to qualify the initial contacts much more rigorously, with the result that in the following year we spent a lot less on generating the same number of clients and released a lot of time for more rewarding activity.

Note here that we were able to modify our strategy because we had gathered and analysed the data about where both our prospects and our clients came from. This is essential for all your marketing activities, whatever system you use to manage your prospects.

Sales statistics

The actual statistics you generate will depend on your sales process, but in principle they should tell you how effective your marketing is in delivering good-value prospects and how effective your sales effort is in converting them into clients. At a minimum, you should know for a given period:

1. Number and source of prospects

2. Number and source of clients

3. Conversion ratio (2 divided by 1)

4. Orders per client

5. Revenue per client

6. Value per order (5 divided by 4)

These various measures and ratios reflect both the effectiveness and the quality of your sales and marketing.

This is not all. The conversion ratio – the number of prospects you need to generate one client or £1,000 of sales – enables you to calculate how many prospects you need every month to achieve your sales goal and therefore what marketing you have to do to generate that number. Once this is established, say ten prospects per month generating two clients worth an average £20K each, you can adjust your marketing and sales strategies to suit. Then you can set about improving each ratio so you can grow the business and your profits without an equivalent increase in time (working smarter not harder) and even spend more time with the family!

One of our clients had such good data on six different marketing activities that we were able to help him calculate not just the number of clients generated per activity, but also the cost of generating them per activity! As a result, he refocused his efforts on two of them, continued with a third and abandoned the other three. It saved him time, heartache and money.

Getting into Retail

At several points in the preceding sections, we mentioned some specific features of marketing and selling into the retail market that differ from the business sector. In this section, we will look more closely at the key elements of marketing and selling successfully to consumers.

This is a huge area, and we limit ourselves to providing an overview of the guiding principles and giving some useful pointers. These principles and pointers have helped many owners of small retail businesses to grow substantially. However, if you find that you need more detailed help, we suggest you approach a specialist on retail marketing in your sector.

The defining feature of the retail market is that your customers come to you, whether your shop is on the high street or the internet. This profoundly affects how you market and sell your products: your customers need to find you easily and you want them to buy from you rather than the shop down the street or the next website on their search list. We will therefore examine the preparation and engagement phases as before, but with special emphasis on how to encourage them to come into your shop and buy.

Preparation

1. Know your product ('what')

It is vital that you can describe accurately and precisely what you are selling. This is important in the business sector too, but the crucial difference is that the customer already knows what the benefit is, so you focus almost entirely on the product itself, such that people of all backgrounds and education will recognise it instantly. You cannot afford the slightest chance of confusion or ambiguity: 'Kitchen Shop' does not tell me whether you sell kitchenware (pots, pans, knives etc.), kitchen equipment (cookers and dishwashers) or kitchens (complete units).

2. Know your market ('who')

Now that your product is clear, who is the intended market? There are many ways to slice and dice, but start with the obvious ones and get more specific until you have a description that fits the majority of your customers: men, women, children? What age range? What level of spending power? What sort of jobs do they do?

3. Know where they are ('where')

Having now identified your target market, where do they live, shop and congregate? If your market is 18–25-year-olds, universities and the entertainment district of town may be the answer; if they are cost-conscious young families, it may be housing estates and out-of-town shopping centres.

The combined information in 2 and 3 is the demographic of your market. The better you know this, the more targeted you can make your engagement strategies and the more successful you will be.

Engagement

4. Know how to reach them ('how')

At the beginning of this chapter (see page 24), we described how your customers exist in one of 5 states. You are now ready to take them from state 1 (unaware) to state 2 (aware). This is not just a matter of the random footfall that happens to walk past your shop; you need to be doing whatever you can to create that footfall and direct it towards your shop or your website (or both).

Your position is equivalent to a crowded market square surrounded by shops. It is not enough to stand behind your counter and wait for people to come in; you need to have someone out there with a billboard, handing out special offers, engaging with people and pointing out the shop as they talk to them.

Your detailed preparations – what you sell, to whom and where they are – now pay off as you can target those people with exactly what they need to know to become aware of you and find you.

Leaflets, local directories, billboards and advertising in magazines, the press, TV and radio all have their part to play, depending on what you are offering and what your budget is, but think carefully where and how your market learns about where they can buy the things they want or need. People in well-to-do areas are more likely to read glossy magazines; those in down-at-heel areas will respond better to leaflets with special deals. A shop on a busy commuter route can catch the attention of passing traffic with a well-designed banner, whereas if it's down a narrow alley off the high street, a billboard chained to a lamp post in the high street will work better.

The customer is now in front of your shop, maybe for the first time. We all know about first impressions, so what impression are they going to get when they see your shop front? Is it clean, attractive, well cared for and welcoming? Is it clear what you are selling? Is there something in the window that will draw people inside?

In addition to these various marketing mechanisms, there is another that can be particularly powerful. Earlier in this chapter (see page 54), we talked briefly about strategic partnerships, but it is in the retail sector that these really come into their own, and in some cases they have evolved into highly sophisticated marketing mechanisms (just think about how supermarkets have come to dominate petrol sales!).

Think carefully about others who serve the same demographic as you and examine what you could offer them to advertise your products and services. Likewise, ask them what they could offer that you could give out to your customers. The precise nature of the arrangement will vary, but ultimately both parties have something to gain by having something extra to offer their customers that sets them apart from their competitors. We may not recognise it, but there are many examples:

- Lands' End, a mail-order clothing retailer, encloses with every order a voucher from Naked Wines, an independent wine merchant, offering £60 off your first purchase of wines.

- Women's magazines have a sheaf of special offers every month from companies eager to do business with their readership.

- A dealer in executive cars offered anyone who took a test drive a voucher for a set of cufflinks, worth £50, to spend at a neighbouring high-quality gents' outfitter. The customer happily dropped into the outfitter to spend their voucher, saw the wonderful range of quality suits and probably finished up buying a shirt and tie as well! Meanwhile, anyone who bought a suit was given a voucher offering an executive car to drive for a day.

  In both cases, the cost to the retailer was minimal and the value to the customer was substantial. How was that for a win-win?

- A shop on the edge of town selling bridal wear found that a high-street jeweller sold more engagement rings at the end of May than at any other time of year. The jeweller happily agreed to display a roll-up banner from the bridal-wear shop, offering a 10% discount on bridal wear for anyone who bought an engagement ring. The advantage for the bridal-wear shop was obvious, but what about the jeweller? There was no point in a reverse offer from the bridal shop because people buy the engagement ring long before they buy the dress. The jeweller was happy because people will look at several shops before choosing their ring and he had something significant to offer that set him apart from other jewellers in the area.

The wedding market offers many opportunities for alliances and partnerships of this sort; it just takes careful thought to ensure everyone benefits and that standards of service and quality are equivalent.

5. Know how to sell to them

Your customer is now at stage 3, when they know and can see what you offer. The interaction is now on a one-to-one basis, but not necessarily with you or your staff yet.

Shop layout/display

The first interaction your customer has is with the goods on display! Are they displayed and the area laid out so people can easily find what they are looking for? This can mean several things:

- Similar products or products that naturally go together are displayed together.

  Armand Thierry, a ladies' fashion chain in France, displayed their clothes in such beautifully matched styles and colour schemes that husbands stood in awe and admiration as their wives happily emptied the bank account.

- Display cabinets and shelves are well lit and accessible.

- Products are well described, if appropriate, and pricing is clear.

- Access is easy and uncluttered.

  A fishing tackle shop was so disorganised and gloomy that even a pleasant assistant couldn't find things; a man and his son made their excuses and went to the more expensive store a short distance away, which had the same floor area but was well lit and laid out logically and spaciously. They bought what they wanted, plus half a dozen other things as well!

These are obvious 'must-haves', but there are other tricks too; if you sell a lot of things that people buy regularly alongside others that are likely to be occasional or impulse buys, try putting the regular stuff at the back of the shop, so shoppers walk past all the other tempting things on the way to buy their regular items and then again on their way back to the till.

Think of all the senses too; smell especially can be very powerful in both attracting and repelling shoppers. It is no coincidence that supermarkets feed the air from the bakery into the air-conditioning outlet at the entrance, nor that the riot of colour from the fresh fruit and veg is the first thing you see when you enter. The milk and bread will be at the back and the chocolate and magazines at the tills. It takes a strong-minded shopper to come out of a supermarket with only what they went in for!

Customer service

This is the real double-edged sword! Get it right and shoppers will love you or at least not desert you. Get it wrong and the whole neighbourhood will hear about it.

The comments earlier in this chapter (see pages 82–86) are really applicable here. You certainly want people coming into your shop or onto your website to have the most positive experience possible. In the interests of making things easy, we will repeat some of the key points from that section, because they are absolutely pivotal:

- **Buying decisions are 80% emotionally based:**

  People will forget what you said,
  People will forget what you did,
  But they will NEVER forget how you made them feel!

  Perhaps this explains some familiar features of customer behaviour:

  ▷ They will relate a bad experience to ten people, but a good experience to only one.

  ▷ One bad experience will wipe out the memory of ten good ones.

  ▷ They probably won't tell you, they just won't come back.

- **Attitude**

  How many times have you been put off by a surly receptionist, a bored cashier or shop assistants chatting to each other instead of serving you?

  You and your staff must have a positive, welcoming attitude. Your customers will respond in kind and it will be much easier to find out what will satisfy them and keep them coming back.

- **Communication**

  Talk to the customer and let them know what is happening, even (in fact especially) if it is bad news. Creating and retaining customer loyalty may not be how you do things when everything's fine, but how you respond when things go wrong.

- **The WOW factor**

  Try doing something out of the ordinary and 'going that extra mile' to make the experience of dealing with you memorable.

  There is a delightful story from a small supermarket in the US. After a pep talk from the manager to all the staff, a young man employed to pack customers' bags thought of putting pleasant little messages on slips of paper in their shopping. He didn't say anything, but prepared them at home and came to work in the morning armed with a bundle of them. After a little while, the staff noticed that some customers were hanging back to pay until they were sure they would be in his line. Business began to creep up as word spread about the witty little messages people found in their shopping when they got home.

- **Know your products**

  You and your staff must have a good understanding of your products. The more specialised your range, the more they need to know, because customers will really appreciate good advice before they buy.

- **Be attentive and available, but don't hound or hover**

  Customers must feel they can talk to you and ask questions, but they also need space and don't want to be pounced on by three sales assistants the moment they walk through the door. Getting this right can be difficult, but just remember you want your customers to have a good experience, and that is what drives your salesperson's commission or your end-of-week target, not a high-pressure selling job!

6. Repeat sales and customer retention

As we stressed above, the more positive your customers' experience, the more likely they are to return. However, there are other things you can do to encourage them to come back, such as loyalty schemes for regular repeat purchases like a meal or groceries. However, if customers are to change their behaviour because of a loyalty scheme, the reward has to be serious and meaningful too. This was the basis for trading stamps many years ago and for Nectar points today.

7. Track and measure

The retail sector is no different to any other when it comes to the necessity of tracking and measuring your marketing effort, as discussed at length in the preceding section (see pages 87–89).

However, the information can largely come from your customers themselves. Discount vouchers and loyalty cards may help drive some extra business your way, but you really should be asking them how and where they heard about you and recording their answers.

Getting into the Public Sector

There are considerable rewards for supplying to the public sector:

- Contracts are usually for 3 years, sometimes longer.

- Payment is prompt and guaranteed.

- It acts as a powerful reference when bidding for other work.

But there are some considerable hurdles to overcome to win the business and there are two key features that must be understood before embarking on this route:

- You must be prepared for several bidding failures before you are likely to win one.

- It is a volume business if any reasonable profits are to be made, as the prices will be very keen and margins slim.

As with the retail sector, our overview of the guiding principles and explanation of the process have helped many small businesses to succeed, but if this is not enough for your needs, you will need to consult a specialist in your field who can advise on the best way to respond to the tender request.

As in all marketing, there is preparation, engagement and evaluation, but with significant differences to everything that we have seen up to now. By understanding what drives the public sector, you will acquire the mindset to work with them and provide what they ask for in the form they need it.

Preparation

The preparation phase is all about understanding what drives commercial decisions in the public sector and gearing up to align yourself with that process.

The public sector, as an arm of government, has to be seen to be scrupulously fair and objective, and will therefore only accept offers in response to a tender. You cannot simply go and meet the county council's purchasing manager and negotiate a deal.

Likewise, the public sector must be seen to follow all legal and recommended commercial processes and requires its suppliers to show they are doing the same. In particular, this means having polices in place covering:

- health and safety
- equal opportunity

- environment

- quality

- business continuity

Contracts are for 3 years, primarily because public sector bodies do not want the expense and effort of doing this every year; they therefore ask to see your accounts for the last 3 years, not to pry into your profits but to be assured that you are established and likely to last the distance. For the same reason, they will want to be sure you have insurances in place that are not just legally required, but enable you to carry on in the case of a claim. Employers' liability and public liability insurance are a must, plus professional indemnity insurance if you are offering any form of consultancy.

If you are offering some other specific services, you may need to demonstrate that you operate to the relevant industry or professional standard and have any other necessary insurance.

Learning about tenders

There are several bodies that advertise tenders on their websites and will continuously update you regarding those in which you have registered an interest.

You can easily overload yourself by applying for all and sundry and not doing any of them justice, so you must be selective. You need to choose those where you can answer the vast majority of likely questions with confidence and give them your very best shot. Be assured that even this will occupy a lot of your time, even when you have all the usual documents and statements to hand!

The engagement phase

The key here is to understand that the tender document is the salesperson!

Every answer has to address not only each question accurately and fully, but also to 'sell' the point. Thus if the question is "Do you have a health and safety policy?" the answer is not simply "Yes". A H&S specialist will be looking at your response later in the assessment and will want to see some evidence that you and your staff know it and apply it in your everyday life. This and other answers like it all build a picture that shows you are established, serious and a good community citizen.

You must also assume that your tender document will be split up and the separate pieces passed to different members of the assessing team. To make this easy for them, you must answer every question fully, even if it means repeating answers from elsewhere in the document. Simply referring the reader to your answer to question 2.1 when answering question 5.1 may well mean that an assessor doesn't get to see your answer and you will be marked down unnecessarily.

The tender document tells you what points are carried per question and the panel awards points accordingly, so in a question worth 10 points, you might get 2 or 3 for a simple Yes, but 8 or 9 for a full answer that shows you understand why they have asked the question.

The price usually accounts for 40–60% of the available points, to show that other aspects of the contract are important too. Your pricing needs to be keen, but if it is too low, the panel may judge that something important will suffer and mark you down as a result.

While you cannot negotiate individually with anyone, the project leader in the public sector body will happily answer clarifying questions and post the answers on the website for all to see.

One question will invariably stump a young business or one that has not worked in the public sector before: 'Provide details of other similar contracts you have completed and of the public sector body that awarded them'. You will either have to price yourself very low and demonstrate that everything else is in place and secure, or you will have to ride on the back of someone else to gain experience before you start bidding in your own right. It is not very satisfactory, but the nature of the public sector is risk averse, in a way that the private sector finds intensely frustrating!

The process

Usually you will have to complete a pre-qualification questionnaire (PQQ) to ensure you have all the necessary policies, procedures, certifications and insurances in place and that it is worth their while spending the time assessing your tender submission. Sometimes the PQQ is longer and more involved than the tender!

They will then send you the tender documents, with full instructions on how to complete them and when and by what means they need to be delivered back. Make very sure you meet the deadline or you will not be considered.

They will then select the top three and invite them to make a presentation to the assessing panel. Now is your chance to sell yourself, by explaining:

- how you will deliver the contract

- how you will take over from the current incumbent

- how you will ensure the project leader will have no problems or issues

- how, and how frequently, you will communicate with the project leader

- how you will treat any employees who you are obliged to take over under TUPE regulations

If you win, it's now a matter of getting installed and up and running, according to your tender and presentation replies.

Bear in mind that the council is obliged to put the contract out to tender again in 3 years' time; your only advantage will be to demonstrate a good track record. If your price puts you second, you will lose it!

If you do not win, you will feel absolutely wretched and drained, so don't deny it, but don't dwell on it either. Rather, ask the council for feedback on your response and presentation so that you can address any weaknesses in your next tender. Sooner or later, if you can stay the distance, you will win!

Private sector tenders

Large corporations will often do their own tendering process. It will operate in much the same way, but will not be as complicated or carry a time limit. The contract will continue until the company decides otherwise, for whatever reason.

Getting New Products and Services

Very few markets stand still or are so satisfied with what they buy today that they are content to stay with it forever. Innovation and development are at the heart of business life; just think back 20 or 30 years and recall (or imagine, if you're that young) what life was like without things that today we take for granted, such as the mobile phone, the internet or cheap flights. By the same token, things that were familiar then are now just distant memories: telex, dial phones, 2-star petrol.

The same is true for services. Then it was the normal order of things to wait 3 months for a phone line; now we expect it in a few days.

The point is that whatever your business, it will evolve. The rate of evolution and innovation will vary from sector to sector, from apparently moribund to breathtakingly fast, but if we are not noting what is happening in the world around us and in our market particularly, we can be left stranded by more observant and nimble competitors.

For small-business owners, who have just got on top of their product or service and worked out how to find their customers and sell to them, this is not welcome news! However, it need not be that frightening if you look at it logically and from your customers' point of view.

You have already thought about your relationship with your clients and know enough about them to know what they are thinking and where they see their business heading. You will know if there are other products or additional services that you can add to your current product line to widen your appeal and, in the process, contribute to growing your own business; you will know what improvements your clients would like to see or what problems they have that could be solved by some development of your product line. You may be proactive and spot something that they don't know they need that could save them money or that would enhance their offering to their marketplace.

The common thread is that you need to carve out time to work on your products and services, establish that any changes or additions are beneficial to both your marketplace and to yourself, and then set about introducing them.

You have now come full circle, as you now have to go back to the beginning of this chapter (see page 24) to work on the description and benefits of your new product, what makes it special and why it is worthwhile for your customers to talk in greater detail with you.

A final note of caution: if your passion is creating things, such as a new widget, a solution to someone's problem or a new training package, you can become so absorbed in your creative heaven that more mundane activities like marketing and selling get pushed aside. The second example in the section on SWOT analysis in Chapter 5 (see pages 171–175) is a classic example, where the managers of the business were so enthralled by the technological challenge of creating products to solve obscure problems that they gave no thought to the fact they had to make enough of them, and do so at some point in the not-too-distant future, to make the development worthwhile!

– Chapter 3 –
Resources and Support Functions

Chapter 3 – Resources and Support Functions

This is one of the three pillars of the organisation that we discussed in Chapter 1 (see pages 14–17) and covers all the activities that enable your business to function smoothly and legally, such as finance, HR, IT, legal and administration processes.

Although each activity is a specialism in its own right, there are two universal truths that apply to all of them, especially as your business grows:

- **Impact on the business** – You need to have a strategy for each one, which you review regularly to ensure that it is still appropriate to your business and its needs.

- **People** – With the probable exception of the smallest business, you will almost certainly need a specialist in the subject to manage it for you: a bookkeeper and accountant for your financial affairs; a HR practitioner to manage the recruitment, training and retention of your people and to ensure compliance with current employment law; an IT specialist who keeps your systems running smoothly and advises on ways to utilise them effectively; and an office manager to ensure the administration of the business runs smoothly and effectively.

  Whether these people are employed or contracted, **they must have the knowledge and skills appropriate to the size and complexity of your business.** Even if you are very small and do some or all these things yourself, you will need the support of people with the knowledge and expertise to advise you when you need it and, perhaps just as importantly, to alert you to what you don't know but need to know!

This chapter consists of the following sections:

- **People** – understanding the day-to-day management of the people who support your business, whether they are employed, freelance or contracted.

- **Finance** – understanding the day-to-day financial management of the business and addressing some common issues.

- **IT (information technology)** – understanding the key factors in getting the most out of your information and communication systems and avoiding common pitfalls that could potentially wreck your business. This means having a system that runs smoothly and securely without interruption, helps to make your business more efficient and provides the right information at the right time to both staff and customers.

- **Premises, plant and equipment** – ensuring you have all the physical assets of the business that you need, in addition to your computers, servers and printers, and that they perform to the standard you require, when you require it.

- **Purchasing and stock control** – ensuring that the business purchases the services, materials and equipment it needs, at the right price and in quantities that balance what you need to operate with the capital tied up in stock.

- **Administration** – ensuring that you have the systems in place for the business to function and grow, and that they operate effectively (they do what they are supposed to do) and efficiently (they do not take up too much of your time).

- **Legal issues** – understanding common legal requirements and issues that affect small businesses, as well as the benefits and protections.

- **Business continuity** – thinking about the unlikely but potentially catastrophic events that could wreck your business, and what you can do to minimise the chance of those things happening, protect yourself and your income from the immediate effects should the worst happen and ensure the business will continue.

People

"There's nowt as strange as folk." – old Yorkshire saying

Introduction

Much as you might prefer it otherwise, you simply cannot operate your business in isolation! Quite apart from the people you sell to, and try to sell to, those you buy from and those you fend off because you don't want to buy from them, there are all those people you engage to help you run the business and perform some of its functions.

The better you understand all those different people and what makes them tick, the more likely you will be able to find the people you can work with successfully, whether you are supplying them or they are supplying you with goods and services, or they are helping you in some capacity to run your business.

While all those different people are vital to your business, this section focuses on the last category – those people you engage to help you do things or to do things on your behalf. This is the function often abbreviated to 'HR', short for human resources. Unlike physical resources, which are designed to do a certain job and generally do it, humans have irritating characteristics like opinions and feelings and require quite different handling to get them to 'do the job'.

Employment law

There is, of course, a large body of law governing employment, some of which is fairly basic and applies to any employer, however small.

This section looks at employment from a practical point of view, to work with people for the good of the business. The section on pages 133–143 looks at this from a legal perspective, discussing an employer's legal requirements regarding issues such as contracts, job descriptions, working conditions and health and safety.

If these are issues of interest and concern to you, we advise you to read both sections and then consider what expert help and advice you need to ensure compliance with the law.

The purpose of HR

The first thing to bear in mind is that an employee will not have the same passion and commitment towards your business as you do, so you cannot expect them to behave, react and give of their own time as you do. The best you can do is to find someone with the right personality, attitude and skills who will fit into the company culture, and to define what is required of them as closely as possible so that everyone is as clear as possible, while leaving room for desirable creativity.

The purpose of HR is therefore threefold: to get the best out of the people who work for you, to protect your interests and to comply with legal requirements.

Some small businesses will immediately say that HR does not apply to them as they do not employ people. What they actually mean is that they do not take them onto the payroll and do not have to comply with employment legislation, but they will almost certainly engage people on a contractual basis to prepare their accounts, to service their IT system, to generate prospects or to do the books. The only difference is the level of compliance with legal requirements; they still want to get the best out of these people and they still need to protect their own interests. We therefore urge you, if you engage anyone as a contractor, to go through the same selection, training and management processes as you would if you were taking them onto the payroll. We will return to the question of 'employee or contractor' later in the section.

The HR process

The HR process is best approached by breaking it down into four stages, corresponding to the periods before, during and after people spend time with you, namely:

1. Recruitment and selection

2. Induction and training

3. Performance management

4. Release (termination or resignation)

1. Recruitment and selection

The very first thing to do is to check that you actually do need to recruit someone in the first place! This may seem a strange way to start, but you need to be sure there is not a better or more economical way to address the reason you are looking for extra help.

Let us assume that you do need someone. The next step is to identify exactly what you want, that is:

- What job needs to be done? What is the role of the person doing it?

- Will it be full-time, part-time, casual or seasonal?

- What sort of skills, knowledge, qualifications, experience and, above all, attitude, are you looking for?

- What are you prepared to pay, either as salary (and add 15–20% for employers' tax and national insurance) or as the cost of a contractor?

- Could it be better or more economically done by a contractor?

The answers to these questions will tell you firstly that you are either sourcing a contractor or recruiting an employee and secondly, the criteria you will use to find them. It is worth creating a checklist of all the elements of the job and whether they are critical 'must-haves' or merely important 'nice-to-haves'. This will make the selection process easier and, if more than one person is involved in the selection, more consistent and transparent.

So far the selection has been based on written answers, which will serve to narrow the field but will not address issues of personality and 'fit' with the company. The next stage is a face-to-face interview, which can be done over the internet if the broadband connection and video quality are good enough. Decide who is going to carry out the interview and, if there will be more than one person, whether they will interview as a panel or in sequence. Having different members of staff meeting candidates can be useful for both parties to decide if there is a good fit. The questions should be consistent and reflect the criteria that appeared in the recruitment material.

Do not be afraid to select no one if none of the candidates meet the criteria. If you have some reservation, you can always offer a temporary contract, to be confirmed within a short period, say 3 months.

Most employment contracts have a probationary period, which both sides can use to confirm that they have made the right choice, but we strongly recommend not using it as an excuse for a cheap dismissal. On the contrary, you want it to work out, so use the period to check often and resolve any concerns.

2. Induction and training

Remember that everything is new and unfamiliar to a new arrival, while existing staff have to stop doing their normal jobs to accommodate them. It is therefore best to have an induction and training plan ready on day one and to share it with the staff who will be working with the new employee. The first day will be taken up with the paperwork, contract and staff handbook, and the next few days understanding the job, meeting colleagues, getting to know the business and learning what is expected of them in their new role.

Some formal training may be necessary, in which case it should be organised as soon as possible, but beware of over-reliance on the 'learn it on the job' approach, which can be a substitute for proper planning and can lead to learning bad habits as well as good ones!

3. Performance management

This follows on from training and is an excellent discipline, whatever size the company is. If properly and intelligently applied, it is an excellent way of making sure you hold on to good people and get the best out of them. In larger companies, it will be managed through a formal appraisal system, in smaller ones more informally through regular and frequent communication.

There will be a number of measures to guide the owner, and the managers if applicable, towards making the company successful. These are called key performance indicators or KPIs. They can reflect results (sales per month) or activity (customer visits per month). If they are carefully chosen, they can be used as targets and incentives for staff, to drive the behaviour that generates the results you want.

If they are used this way, it is important that:

- they are in the individual's control, so they can be held accountable for them

- they are agreed with the individual

- they are consistent across all staff

- they are reviewed regularly, at least once per quarter, with every individual

- any issues arising are 'nipped in the bud'

This last point applies generally, but it is surprising how many managers sweep issues under the carpet or just flatly deny they exist, rather than address and deal with them. As in families and life at large, an unaddressed problem in the workplace can fester and grow out of all proportion, like an abscess under the skin, until it either reaches crisis point and explodes or becomes a chronic condition that is simply accepted as the standard. Either way, and especially in a small business, staff relations will suffer, closely followed by the business.

Many owners and managers struggle with the idea of 'rewards and recognition', thinking it's just about more money. In fact, it's about what motivates people to do more and do better, to offer their time and apply their talents to improve the business. It requires managers to get to know their people and understand what makes them tick, and to apply that little something (not necessarily money) that shows you have noticed what they have done and are thanking them for it in a way that is meaningful for them. Earlier we said that you cannot expect your staff to share your passion and commitment for the business, but this is an excellent way to bring them somewhere close.

Staff morale and good communication usually go hand in hand. Whether the news is good or bad, frequent communication, in both directions, is essential to getting the best out of people, irrespective of the size of the company. A useful tip in communicating with staff is that, just as with talking to prospects and customers, we have two ears and one mouth and should use them in the same proportion.

4. Release

This is a general term covering the different ways a member of staff may leave the company. Release can occur as the result of:

- dismissal following a disciplinary procedure (conduct, capability)

- dismissal through poor performance (capability, attitude)

- redundancy (the job itself is disappearing, but you cannot then recruit someone to fill it the next week!)

- resignation (the employee's choice, but there may be terms, such as not working for a competitor for a certain length of time; it can be helpful also to conduct an exit interview)

- retirement (remember that you cannot now require someone to retire simply because they have reached a certain age)

Family businesses

These can be very successful or they can be fraught with difficulty. This can be for a variety of reasons, such as the relationships in the business becoming interwoven with the personal relationships in the family, or the individual responsibilities and expectations not being clearly defined.

We would always recommend that family businesses have individual agreements, like any other business, that clearly define responsibilities, accountability and expectations. The role that non-family members may play or can be expected to play should also be very clearly defined.

Employee or contractor?

It is normal and sensible to employ specialist contractors to do one-off or occasional jobs that you or your staff cannot do easily or without distracting you or them from their proper jobs. Likewise, a contractor can carry out a project for you that may or may not involve your staff, such as conducting some market research or a telemarketing campaign.

But what about regular, routine jobs? Having considered all the issues involved in recruiting, retaining and releasing staff, you may well be wondering whether it's worth all the hassle. Would it not be cheaper, quicker and simpler just to employ a contractor to do the same thing? After all, if they don't work out, you can simply terminate the contract like any other commercial agreement and find someone else.

For very small businesses, the cost, flexibility and simplicity of using an independent contractor to do vital things like bookkeeping, telephone answering and appointment setting make perfect sense. It is a simple commercial transaction that can be adjusted or terminated very easily, subject to the conditions of the agreement, and there is little in the way of legal regulation to worry about. Recruitment is simpler too; you would probably use your business networks to find the resource that suits you and comes with a recommendation or testimonials from other clients. Finally, there should be no need to train the contractor: you are employing them because they know how to do the job!

However, as the business grows, so the cost will rise as you use the contractor more often. A contractor's day rate is likely to be significantly higher than the wage of an employee doing the same job because they have to take care of all their own tax, national insurance, sickness benefits, pension contributions and so on, as well as covering their marketing and administrative costs. At some point, the cost of the contractor will outweigh the cost and hassle of employing someone.

An equally significant issue as the business grows is commitment. A half-decent contractor will probably have other clients and commitments, and they may not always be able or willing to fit in with your schedule if you start to need them for significant chunks of their week or month. A contractor works to the agreement and probably a friendly relationship will develop, but in the end it is just a commercial arrangement. If you employ someone for a certain number of hours per week, they are obliged to work those hours exclusively for you and at the times of day you have agreed. If you have chosen wisely and manage them well, the employee will become more closely associated with your business and may even start to feel part of it, which is when you start to get the best out of them!

In the end it is a balancing act, depending on what you want done and how you feel about managing people and all that entails. However, whichever route you go down, once they are on your premises they will need guidance and unambiguous instruction over what you want and expect, and reassurance that they can expect respectful treatment in return.

Health and safety (H&S)

The requirements are largely covered in the section on pages 133–143, but from a management point of view, involving your associates, employees and regular contractors in keeping the workplace safe can be a very useful way of improving communication and staff morale.

Workplace safety is a joint responsibility between employer and employee. You have a responsibility to provide a safe environment, develop safe working practices and ensure everyone on your premises knows the rules and follows them. The employee and anyone else on your premises, whether working or visiting, has a reciprocal responsibility to understand, accept and follow all safety rules and instructions. This is primarily a behavioural issue, in that accidents occur and people get hurt when they are unaware of hazards, don't notice them or choose to ignore them.

The best way to make sure your staff follow your rules and stay safe all the time, and not just when you are watching, is to involve them, both in assessing the hazards and risks and in developing the rules and working practices to control them. They will then understand why the rules are there and take ownership of them. This will have a beneficial effect on the rest of the business too: you will feel more confident in involving them in other parts of the business and benefitting from their knowledge and input, and they will feel closer and more committed to the business.

This is a shining example of doing what you have to do, but in such a way that you achieve a primary objective: to get the best out of your people!

Finance

"Annual income twenty pounds, annual expenditure nineteen pounds nineteen and six, result happiness. Annual income twenty pounds, annual expenditure twenty pounds ought and six, result misery."
David Copperfield (Charles Dickens)

Now we come to the part on which every business stands or falls – finance. If your business was a human body, production would be the heart, the board would be the brain, sales and marketing would be the arms and legs and finance would be the blood!

Just like blood in the body, if the finances are healthy and strong, the rest of the body can function as it should. If blood is weak and anaemic, the body weakens and starts shutting down, until eventually even the vital organs fail. We can all think of businesses that have done exactly that.

As in life generally, so in business: finance behaves simultaneously as an enabler (allows you to do things), a constraint (but only so many at a time!) and a measure of progress and success. It is therefore vital for your business, whether large or small, that you manage the flow of finance into and out of the company to ensure it stays healthy, to enable you to meet all your business obligations and to provide you with a return appropriate to your effort and investment.

In this section we will look at ways the owner of a small business can control its finances without needing an accounting qualification or fancy software, and at what point to employ the services of a suitably qualified accountant. We will then look at some common financial issues directly related to the day-to-day running of the business and ways of identifying and dealing with their root causes.

Your bank account

The very first thing that needs to be said is that you must have a separate business bank account, even if you are a sole trader or a very small one-person business.

The next thing is that you must conduct all your business dealings through your business bank account, even if some of it is done in cash! It is then much easier to reconcile what is going in and out with your paperwork; if you muddle your personal and business expenses, you can get in a hopeless mess. On top of that, the taxman may make assumptions about your business that appear grossly unfair but which you will be unable to contest because you do not have the evidence.

We also recommend that if you use a credit card for business expenses, keep it only for business expenses and have a separate one for personal use. It is so much easier to keep track!

Counting the beans – bookkeeping and accounts

Bookkeeping

Bookkeeping is the maintenance of detailed records of income and outgoings, organised in such a way that it provides useful information for the running of the business and for the calculation of tax at the end of the company's financial year. For the smallest business, this need be no more than a record of invoices issued and paid and of bills received and paid, including receipts for incidental expenses, and this can be perfectly well done on a spreadsheet. For larger businesses with a more complex organisation, bookkeeping software becomes necessary to keep finances under control.

Whether you do this yourself or engage a professional bookkeeper, it is essential to do it properly and regularly, both to enable you to manage the business and to enable your accountant to prepare your tax return. The easier you make it for them, the less excuse they will have to charge you a fortune!

If you handle cash in your business, either received from customers in payment (a retail business, for example) or paid out to suppliers, it must all be properly accounted for. It is easy, especially for very small businesses, to lose track of it unless they are very careful to keep it separate from the loose change in their pockets! In retail businesses, where you have to entrust staff with handling it, a daily reconciliation is essential, both to satisfy the taxman and to ensure that none is inadvertently going walkabout.

Management accounts

Good bookkeeping organises your financial data and converts it into financial information that enables you to see if you are proceeding according to plan and to take decisions about spending, investment, growth, marketing and so on. Management accounts are the outcome: your financial data is expressed and presented in a way that enables you to understand how the business is performing and what needs to happen to ensure you stay on track and achieve your goal.

The taxman, your tax return and your accountant

Unfortunately, the taxman looks at your business rather differently. He is only interested in how much taxable profit you have made. He determines this from the tax return you have to submit each year and, unless you are a very small business, you will almost certainly need a qualified accountant to prepare it. This is not all bad: an accountant makes sure you are not only complying with, but also taking advantage of, the byzantine rules that govern taxation. This really is a specialised field that does not always follow logical thought patterns, so it is worth investing in a good accountant who takes an interest in your business and understands how the shifting sands of tax legislation will affect you, for better or worse, and ensures you comply with the various deadlines that HMRC impose. Our own experience suggests that the fee you pay your accountant is more than offset by various obscure elements that they can legitimately apply to lower your tax liability.

Many accountants will happily offer to do your bookkeeping as part of their service. Just be aware that they are almost certainly subcontracting it to a bookkeeper and charging an oncost for doing so.

VAT or not

In 2013/14, the threshold at which you have to register for and pay VAT is £77,000 per year, so the first question is whether you are well below or well above this level.

If you are not registered for VAT, your bookkeeping is simpler and you do not have to make monthly or quarterly returns to HMRC. However, if you plan to grow your business to near or above the threshold, you really should register straight away and get used to it. This is especially true if your business involves selling to the public; we worked with one retail business that was not VAT registered but as the business grew, it became clear that it would have to register when turnover sailed past the threshold. This presented it with a pricing dilemma, as it now had to extract the 20% VAT from every sale and return it to the taxman!

Even if you are doing your own books, it's not that difficult or complex, and with proper organisation and online submission of your VAT return, it is quite quick too. Just make sure to keep a hard copy of your VAT records, as your accountant will need to verify them when preparing your tax return.

There are other advantages to being VAT registered. The obvious one is that you reclaim VAT on the majority of your business purchases, but also as a VAT-registered business you come over as a sizeable, and therefore a more credible, business.

Limited or sole trader

This is a subject for discussion with your accountant, if you have any doubt which is better for you. There are advantages and disadvantages to both arrangements, but we would suggest that in general, being limited does not just limit your liabilities, but also lends credibility and weight to your enterprise.

The universal financial complaint

This may be expressed in many ways, but they all come down to a single cry of anguish:

"I haven't got enough money."

This is the outcome either of a failure to generate sufficient income or to control outgoings, or a combination of both. Insufficient income means insufficient sales, which itself can be, as discussed in earlier sections, a sales or marketing issue or it could be a quality or reputation issue that is preventing people from buying.

We are going to assume that the problem is none of these: you have enough customers buying a product or service that they are happy with and yet things are still not right. In our experience, this can be summarised in one or two questions that we hear over and over again.

1. How come I'm working all hours and making no money?

There can be various reasons for this, such as managing time badly, targeting the wrong audience or not closing deals, but what if it appears that you're doing everything right and it's still not working?

It's rather brutal, but we have to be cruel to be kind. You might be a 'busy fool' – in one of three ways.

Pricing

Especially when small businesses are new on the scene and have yet to develop a reputation, they can be desperately keen to secure orders and find the quickest and simplest way is to price themselves below everyone else; funnily enough, buyers seem to sense that and take full advantage!

Unfortunately, cutting the price can leave you with no profit. Making a habit of it, or allowing your customers to think this is the 'right' price level, is just storing up trouble for the future, and no matter how hard you work or how many hours you put in, you will not make any money.

You must know how much money you need to earn to cover all your costs and allow you to live, and you must know how much it costs to make and deliver a product or prepare and deliver a service. Remember that the time you spend marketing and selling is also a cost that has to be factored into your calculation. Now you can ensure that you price your services properly and are getting a just reward for your efforts. If you are not competitive, then something has to give: either cut your costs (but without starving the vital organs), find a way to sell your special value at a higher price or both. For more about pricing, it may be worth your while to look again at the information in Chapter 2 on pricing (see pages 32–34) and on presenting it to your customer (see pages 79–80).

Selling to the wrong customers

If your customers simply will not pay more because they can get an inferior product that does the job just as well, you are selling to the wrong customer. If the customer is a continuous complainer or promises the earth and delivers peanuts, both of which can soak up your time and energy, you are selling to the wrong customer.

It is essential to go back to basics here and revisit the information at the beginning of Chapter 2 (see page 24) on marketing to establish exactly what makes your product or service special, assess the value it brings to the right sort of customer, price it accordingly, then market directly and specifically to them.

If, after all that, they still mess you about, use the 'three strikes and you're out' rule: after the third time, tell them to approach you if and when they're ready, meanwhile you won't bother them again!

Not controlling your costs

This may seem obvious, but can be misleading. You will have obvious outgoings that may have some room for negotiation downwards, or you may incur costs on things that are nice to have but are not absolutely essential.

You may also have unnecessary costs if your marketing is wrong; not only the cost of the marketing itself, but your time and, possibly, travel costs in attending to it. You have to spend some time and money, or a combination of the two, on your marketing, but it has to be delivering the prospects that you can convert into customers; otherwise it will be consuming all those hours and generating no money in return!

We have already hinted at it, but also take care not to cut costs so drastically that activities that are vital to the health of the business reduce or stop altogether. It can be very tempting to reduce your marketing to save money, but how else are you going to generate the business that will pay the bills?

When looking at cutting costs, please be sure to distinguish between the must-haves and the nice-to-haves and then find the most economical way to acquire the must-haves.

2. How can my business be profitable, yet I never have any money?

This is also a common problem and goes to the heart of the difference between profit and cash flow. Sadly, it is perfectly possible for a business to be profitable, but have no cash to pay its day-to-day bills (or even worse, that massive tax bill it wasn't expecting).

This is because profit is a calculated figure: it is what's left over when the cost of producing and selling something is subtracted from the price it is sold for. It can be calculated for a single product or service or for all the products and services a company sells.

Unfortunately, it is not quite as simple as it sounds. Some costs are fixed; that is you have to pay them whether you sell anything or not. Some costs occur long before the money comes back from selling the product, or you think you have money in the bank when actually it is due to go out later. Other obligations, such as repaying debts, can also soak up the cash you have in the bank!

In our experience, there are two common causes of cash-flow problems; one is entirely under your own control; the other, depending on circumstances, you may be able to influence but may just come with the territory.

Invoices – get them out and get them paid!

It can be as simple as that! A surprising number of small businesses do not have a robust system to get their invoices out regularly and promptly to their customers. Everyone, including you, pays against an invoice. You cannot expect your customers to pay if they do not have the invoice in front of them telling them what, how and when to pay. You must then also have a system to ensure they pay on the due date. You cannot afford to let them keep your cash when you need it!

For more comments on this crucial piece of administration, see the section on pages 130–133, and on terms and conditions and credit control, see pages 136–139.

Timing

If you have to buy materials first, pay people to make the product, store it for a while, then wait 30 days until your customer pays you, you will have laid out all the cost of production long before you get it back. If the customer delays payment, it makes matters worse.

Your transactions have to be profitable, of course, but you must also have the cash available to pay for things when you need them. This is 'working capital' and applies to small businesses just as much as, or perhaps even more than, large ones.

It is common in some trades to require a customer to pay part or all upfront, for example to provide the cash to pay for materials before the job starts. Some larger companies manage to persuade their suppliers to keep stock on their premises and pay for it only when they use it. (This system is called 'consignment stock'; it works well if you are the customer, not so well if you are the supplier!)

It is really important to understand the sequence of events in your particular business and know exactly when money has to be paid out and when you can expect to receive it. For a small business, it is generally much more effective to manage finances day to day based on cash flow rather than on a profit-and-loss statement, and this is why we insist on our clients having a cash-flow record and projection. This will then alert you to potential cash problems well in advance, when you can do something about them. You definitely do not want the first inkling of trouble to be an unpleasant letter from the bank!

Other obligations

This is the difference between operations and the rest of the business. The obvious ones are VAT (usually building up over 3 months), corporation tax (even worse – building up over 12–18 months) and loan repayments. There may be other things, specific to your business.

The key is to recognise them and allow for them, not just in your cash-flow sheet but also in practice. As soon as a customer pays your invoice, or as part of your month-end routine, separate the VAT element and put it in another account; likewise, as you calculate your net profit for a month, calculate 22% of it and put it in another account. This discipline ('accrual') is proper business practice and does two things: it ensures you see only what cash you have to spend and you know you will have the cash available when the VAT return is due or the tax bill arrives.

Summary

For a small business, it really is essential to maintain a cash-flow sheet that tells you instantly what cash you expect to receive and when; and what you expect to pay out and when. It must also include every sort of expenditure the business has to fund – not just raw materials and overheads, but VAT, tax, loans and anything else.

This will also help you make informed decisions about future spending – both the amount and the timing. Not only that, but more immediately it will tell you what level of sales you must generate to meet your obligations and generate the lifestyle you aspire to!

IT

It is worth considering for a moment just how dependent we are on IT and how much it supports and enables just about everything we do:

- Communication: email, social media, VOIP phones, Skype and equivalents, word processing (letters, reports etc.)

- Administration: bookkeeping, accounts, payroll, VAT and PAYE returns, invoicing, customer data

- Marketing: contact and prospect databases, social media, websites, presentations, blogs, online groups

- Management information: business analyses, historical data, financial data and reports

It is perhaps not often that we consider IT in this light, but when we do we realise how powerful and useful it can be and also how much damage could be caused by the loss or theft of our data or equipment.

This therefore raises a number of significant pointers when thinking about how we manage IT in our businesses and particularly how it needs to change as the business grows.

Equipment and infrastructure

Your physical assets such as desktop and laptop computers, printers and mobile phones need to be appropriate to your business needs. That means powerful enough to run the company's software quickly and smoothly, and robust enough to survive normal business use for a reasonable time.

Your infrastructure must be capable of handling the volume of business data, with room to spare, at all times of the business day. In particular, your internet broadband connection, whether wired or wireless, is the business's umbilical cord connecting it to the outside world. It must be fast and robust, as well as reasonably priced.

Software and applications

These provide tremendous opportunities to speed up routine or repetitive operations. Again, they must be appropriate to your business needs and capable of absorbing growth, up to a point. Just be aware that as the business grows, more specialised software will be needed to handle the greater complexity and volume of data, and more licences will be needed as more and more users are added.

Security

The astonishing power and convenience of modern IT systems are not just wonderful for us, but also for those who would do us harm. It is not just our data that the hackers are after. In fact, for a small business, the data is probably not worth much; it is the remote access to, and control of, your computers that enables them to conduct much larger cybercrimes, be they theft or vandalism.

The protection of our systems comes down to three things: awareness, common sense and basic safeguards:

- Ensure you use strong passwords (mix upper and lower case, numbers and symbols) and have a system to remember them that is equally strong (a sticky note stuck to the screen is not recommended. Yes, we have seen it!).

- Have good internet security software that is kept up to date automatically.

- Install the regular software updates.

- Treat any communication that you don't recognise with suspicion. Under no circumstances open email attachments or click web links until you are absolutely sure they are genuine. If by chance you do so, immediately isolate your computer and have it checked by an expert you trust.

- Assume the worst can happen! If you should lose your data because your laptop blows up or because you leave it on a train, you can immediately retrieve your data from your backup. You do run regular backups, of course? Whether you have a second hard disk plugged in that updates continuously or use an online backup service, **you must do it!**

Support and maintenance

Prevention is better than cure! Treat your IT system like your car; have it regularly serviced by people who are competent and skilled to work on your particular model and who will react fast enough when something goes wrong.

Some years ago in a former life, a colleague, Paul, was very proud of his BMW 730, but he also always took the cheapest option, including having his car serviced by the local garage 'down the road', run by a rally driver and ex-Ford mechanic. On one occasion I drove it, and Paul told me to ignore the red light on the panel as it had been there a while and the garage could not find anything wrong. It was a miracle nothing happened because when it was checked by a proper BMW garage, it turned out to be a warning that the brakes were about to fail!

It is really important to work with people, whether employed or contracted, who have the knowledge, skills, experience and capacity to work on your systems. Get testimonials and references, if necessary, from people of similar size to you.

Cloud computing

This is another generic term that has become popular in recent years. In essence, it means that your data is stored and processed in a remote data centre and not on your own hard drive or server.

The benefits are that you need much less storage on your hardware and your data is protected from loss or damage. However, it also means that whenever you need to access it, you must have an internet connection that can handle the speed and volume you would expect from your hard drive, and as we know that will not always be the case!

For small businesses, having email hosted 'in the cloud' can make a lot of sense as it is generally robust and fast, and for a small number of users the cost is very reasonable. However, as the business grows, the extra costs may start to make a local solution more cost-effective.

Discipline

If your business employs staff, it is worth having a policy on IT use and making sure they understand it, accept it and comply with it. This is not just about whether people use your computers to access their Facebook page or play games in work time, although that can be an issue. More serious is the extra risk that viruses or other nasties can be imported into your system, which is more likely through social media activity than from strictly business access.

The other element that is becoming more and more serious as time passes is the libellous effect that employees' Facebook posts can have. People, and especially younger people, can give remarkably little thought to the impact of their words on both themselves and others; what seems to be a witty, harmless comment about the boss at 2 a.m. after a good night out can turn out to be anything but at 9 a.m. in the office!

Your policy on this must be reasonable but firm and you must apply it consistently.

IT strategy

All the points we have covered should be wrapped up in your IT strategy. Larger businesses have whole sections of their management systems devoted to 'management of change'. Most people instinctively think this is about people, but it also covers changes to procedures, plant, materials and, of course, the impact on the company's IT systems.

Your strategy should look at the risk and consequence of data interruption and loss, which will lead to strategic decisions on investment in:

- suitable equipment

- ongoing support

- the service level agreement (what you get and how quickly)

Premises, Plant and Equipment

These encompass the physical resources a business may employ to make its products available for sale and able to be delivered to the customer.

For many small businesses, these may be as simple as some basic office furniture and equipment in a home office; for others, they may be a factory with office space, machinery, packaging equipment, warehousing and vehicles. IT equipment is, of course, a part of this, but IT has such a wide impact on the business that it is treated separately in the previous section (see pages 123–127), although much of what was said there with respect to equipment will apply equally here.

For our purposes in this section, we are interested in two issues: do you buy or lease, and how do you manage maintenance, repair and replacement.

Buy or lease?

This could be summed up in one pithy statement: if it depreciates, lease it; if it appreciates, buy it!

For many small businesses, the cost of buying premises is way beyond what the business can support and just makes no sense at all. A vast number of service businesses are run from a home office (which costs nothing, but can have other problems) or from a modest 1- or 2-room office rented by the month or on a short-term lease. This is both cost-effective and infinitely flexible.

If machinery is involved at all, the same argument can apply, but we have seen businesses where the building was leased but the equipment was owned, and bought and sold when necessary. The arguments for leasing can be very persuasive:

- Predictable and steady cash flow

- Capital not tied up

- Maintenance and quick repair can be included

- Regular replacement and upgrade (equipment)

- Services included (premises)

The main arguments in favour of ownership are:

- There is some asset value if and when the business is sold or a loan needs to be guaranteed.

- You are in control of your own destiny: short-term leases may not be renewed, or the terms may change at each renewal or at very short notice.

- Well-maintained equipment can function for many years and recoup its cost versus leasing many times over.

The decision will come down to individual circumstances, such as the size of the company, its financial position, the impact and likelihood of significant technological change and even the personal preference of the owner.

Maintenance, repair and replacement

We believe all equipment should be regularly maintained, either by the manufacturer, a designated expert or your own staff (provided they have the knowledge and skill, otherwise they can do more harm than good).

Some pieces of equipment are more critical to a business than others, so there needs to be a plan in place to manage the situation if they should fail. Older equipment has a habit of breaking down more often, and sometimes catastrophically, so you should be planning for its replacement or refurbishment before it does you serious damage, especially if you cannot replace it quickly. This is not just for manufacturing; many service businesses rely completely on their laptops, mobile phones and cars, and the same common-sense approach is necessary for them!

Purchasing and Stock Control

If you run a simple service business, these can be a very simple function, involving nothing more than ensuring there is stationery in the cupboard when you need it. If you run a manufacturing company, you will be acquiring raw materials and parts to make your finished products and possibly parts to ensure your plant and equipment run smoothly and without interruption. In this case, the way you do your purchasing and manage your stock can have a critical bearing on the cost and quality of your finished product and your ability to deliver at the time and in the quantity the customer wants it.

Your bookkeeping will be telling you where your major items of expense lie and therefore where you should be focusing your efforts to control your costs most effectively. For the majority of small businesses, this may be phones, travel and marketing; for larger businesses, the fixed or indirect costs of premises and staff and the direct costs of materials and perhaps sales commissions will be more significant.

If your business relies heavily on very short delivery times, the management of your distribution, work flow and stock levels and your relationship with suppliers will all be critical to ensuring your customer is never left short or your competition is never given the chance to muscle in. In this situation, your purchasing and stock control are fully integrated with your entire work-flow planning in what may be a fairly sophisticated operation.

There can be a hidden trap here if you promise short delivery times to win the business and rely on large stocks of finished product or raw materials, or both, to ensure you never run out of anything. Those stocks are sitting there, doing nothing except tying up a lot of cash. If you are a small business, there can be a real danger that this will starve you of the funds you need to run the business.

If you are in this position, you may be able to negotiate with your suppliers to buy on a consignment basis, where you hold the stock but only pay when you actually use the goods. This effectively puts the onus of holding the stock on your supplier, who may be able to absorb the cost much more easily than you can. Using this technique, the owners of a small restaurant we knew were able to offer a huge range of wines and use it as their USP.

Administration

'Administration' is a very long word to write and to say – five whole syllables, in fact. So we are going to make this easier and shorten it to its commonly used form: admin.

It's safe to say that the majority of business owners do not enjoy admin! But like it or not, admin is the oil that keeps the wheels of your business moving. It covers a variety of activities including daily tasks, such as answering the phone, dealing with post and emails and greeting visitors at reception; regular tasks such as quotations, invoices and reports; and occasional but vital paperwork such as company files and legal documentation.

So if it's so vital, why do business owners hate it so much? Perhaps it is because admin is characterised by logical processes, standardised working and attention to detail, whereas the entrepreneurial mind prefers to race to the end point, taking whatever shortcuts it can along the way. If forced to do it, as many small-business owners are, they struggle to do it efficiently and find it tedious and time-consuming when they really want to be out there, doing things!

Recognising that this may not be the section that really gets your pulse racing, we suggest you adopt a logical approach to keep the admin as concise as possible. If you identify the key tasks associated with each block of activity in your organisation, you can then decide who does them, how often and how they are done to make them as straightforward and efficient as possible.

Before getting into the detail, it is worth commenting on how important it is that people do the same admin task in the same way as each other, every time, in order to achieve the same result. This applies just as much to the simplest businesses; how many times have you, or someone you were talking to, 'lost' that vital piece of paper just when it was needed?

There are a number of elements to this, for example:

- using preprinted forms that prompt people to supply the relevant information in a format that others can recognise and use

- ensuring they understand the form so they use it properly and it delivers the intended result

- designing logical filing systems so people know where to put things and where to find them, whether hard copy or electronic

- creating a set of procedures, by writing down the way things are done and checking that people always do them that way

- creating a checklist of tasks in the right sequence for multi-step routines like end-of-month closing and using it to check that the complete routine is done with no omissions

This may seem arduous and bureaucratic, but like several features of business life, once it is done and in operation, it makes life so much simpler and more likely to be 'right, first time'.

Let us therefore revisit your organisation's blocks of activity again to see some of the principal admin tasks that make their wheels go round. Note how some tasks are most easily identified by the forms that are used to conduct them or the resulting reports or agreements.

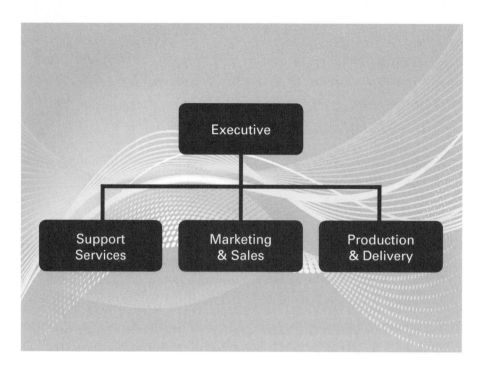

Support services

- Finance: bookkeeping, financial reports, VAT returns

- HR: employment and H&S policies, employment contracts, job descriptions, staff handbooks, training records, performance appraisals, time sheets

- Purchasing: requisitions, purchase orders

- IT: maintenance checklist, email

- Admin: procedures manual, ISO documentation, admin checklists, telephone answering, distributing the post, receiving visitors

Marketing and sales

- Sales board

- Appointment confirmations (email, letter)

- Proposals/quotations/estimates

- Order acknowledgements

- Invoices

- Statements and late payment letters

- Contracts

Production and delivery

- Goods received notes, stock cards, requisitions

- Production schedules, production reports

- Process and quality assurance sheets

- Delivery schedules

- Customer feedback (complaint) forms

Executive

- Management accounts

- Long-term and short-term planning documents

- Management and directors' meeting agendas and minutes

- Legal documentation

- Directors' contracts and agreements

Legal Issues

"Forewarned is forearmed." – English proverb

There are several aspects of business covered in other sections that have a legal as well as a commercial angle to them. Generally, it will not affect you, but it is important to know both what your legal obligations are (to avoid the risk of falling foul of the law) and what your legal rights are (to protect yourself and your business).

This section looks at what these legal elements of business mean. For the most part, the law either lays down a minimum standard that you must meet or covers how to resolve a dispute. By themselves, these will not be enough to run your business successfully; they are there to provide a framework to protect you and other parties as everyone goes about their daily business.

Please, therefore, do not take the information in this section as all you have to do to manage staff or get your money on time; that is what the other sections are for! This section is simply to ensure you operate within the law, to make you aware of the protections it offers and to alert you to possible legal implications for which you need to get expert advice.

If the worst happens…

We have to make it completely clear that if you ever get embroiled in a legal dispute, you absolutely must get expert legal advice and, if necessary, proper legal representation.

We hope that such a situation will never arise, if for no other reason than the time, energy and mental stamina it will demand that should be focused on running your business. For that reason alone, it is worth taking steps to minimise the chance of legal disputes.

At this point we recognise that you may already be losing the will to live. Just bear in mind that the primary reason we can trade successfully and with confidence is that there is a body of law, built up over centuries, that underpins and enforces business agreements. We may laugh about it and 'do anything to avoid getting lawyers involved', but when you are on the receiving end of a rogue or incompetent trader, you will be very glad you have legal rights that can be enforced, in most cases at relatively little expense.

What do we need to know?

We suspect that far more business disputes arise through ignorance and incompetence than through negligence or deliberate wrongdoing. The law addresses all these causes, effectively requiring us to know not just what we need to do, but also to be able and organised to do it to an acceptable standard and to promote our business, products and services fairly and accurately.

So what should the owner of a small or medium-size business be expected to know and do to 'stay legal' and avoid getting caught up in costly legal proceedings? This is not just about compliance; it is also about everyone having a clear understanding of how things will be organised and carried out, especially when things change or go wrong. Generally, we manage this with goodwill, common sense and a shared desire to resolve matters in a friendly way, but we cannot take that for granted, so it is reassuring to know that if something goes wrong or a dispute arises, there are things in place that enable us to resolve it.

Some things may seem obvious but others may surprise you, so it is a good idea to check them out and, if you have any doubts about whether they apply to you, get expert advice.

To stay organised and relevant to the rest of the book, we will look at those topics where there are important legal implications of some sort.

1. Business organisation

Your trading identity

Both your customers and HMRC must know your trading identity. The majority of small businesses will either be sole traders or private limited companies, but there are other constructions. The point is that third parties are entitled to know whether they are dealing with an individual (sole trader), a limited company or some other entity, as each has a different liability. Whichever you are, your company correspondence, emails and website must all show the name of the trading entity and an address to which correspondence may be sent. You will obviously include your email address and phone numbers so people can find and contact you, but they are not a legal requirement.

Internal rights and liabilities

Many small businesses consist of partners or co-directors, who came together to bring their separate areas of expertise to the enterprise. When everyone is enthusiastic and raring to go, the last thing on their minds is how to end it. We can only implore them to establish a proper agreement for every partner or director that sets out what the company expects of them, what they can expect from the company, how ownership is allocated, how profits are assigned and the mechanism for changing or terminating the agreement. Forcing people to think through these different aspects of the business may seem picky and time-consuming, but it will save a huge amount of time and bad feeling later.

2. Sales and marketing

The contract and terms and conditions

An agreement between two parties involving an exchange of something of value constitutes a legally binding contract. There is nothing exceptional in that, but legally the seller must be able and competent to deliver the product or service, and the product or service must be of satisfactory quality and fit for purpose. Some services, such as financial, accounting and legal, are governed by professional standards and the providers must be professionally qualified to offer them, but many rely on the reputation and track record of the provider to assure the buyer of the seller's competence.

A contract can be verbal, but for obvious reasons that is not easy to enforce. It is therefore good practice to record the details of the agreement in writing and, if possible, to have both parties sign it as a formal recognition of their mutual acceptance. In practice, this doesn't often happen, especially with contracts of relatively low value, but even so it is always advisable to provide your customer with a written summary of what you are supplying and under what conditions.

Some of these conditions will be the same for every transaction and some will be specific to individual transactions. Those that are the same can be grouped and standardised into your general terms and conditions, which should accompany every order confirmation and invoice you provide.

They do not have to be complicated, but should limit your liability, protect you from legal action if things change outside your control, exclude third parties from any rights in the contract and state that ownership of goods is retained until they are paid for. Even if you feel your terms cover these points, it is wise to have a solicitor check them. It is best to benefit from everyone else's experience of what makes good commercial sense before you need it, rather than after!

Most 'T&Cs' are written to favour the seller. For this reason, many established businesses have purchase terms and conditions on the back of their purchase orders, which nullify or contradict just about every one of the sales terms and conditions of their suppliers! For the most part, we all just live with this inherent ambiguity and let the lawyers deal with it if it ever comes to the crunch. Just make sure your customer receives a copy of your terms and conditions. If they do not challenge or repudiate them, or any part of them, before you deliver the service, they are deemed to have accepted them and are legally bound by them.

Bearing this in mind, you should always check your supplier's terms and conditions when purchasing supplies or stock. If there is anything in there you don't like, challenge it and agree on an alternative. If you don't, you are bound by their terms and conditions!

Things are rather different if you deal with consumers or the public in a retail business, and here you will probably need to take advice. In general, the law acknowledges and accepts that Joe Public cannot be expected to have the same level of commercial or legal knowledge as you do, so your terms and conditions must be seen to be fair to the consumer. If, as a small trader, you don't have formal terms and conditions, for example if you are selling on a market stall, you will be bound by general consumer law, and even if you have terms and conditions, you must comply with it.

Intellectual property (IP) and copyright

IP is regarded as an asset with a defined value belonging to you or your company and is protected in much the same way as physical property. It can cover any sort of creative work, including articles, systems of work, inventions, trademarks, design rights and patents. This means that no one else can copy it or use it without your express permission and, of course, neither can you copy or use other people's IP without their express permission. Where your IP confers a commercial advantage, you are very unlikely to permit other people to use it unless you decide for another reason to let people do so. This may be for a fee (a licence, for example) or provided your name is acknowledged as the author or owner, thus promoting you or your business.

You are reading an example of that right now! Much of the material in this section comes from two sources of expertise that we gratefully acknowledged at the beginning of the book.

Your website

There are both compliance and protection issues here.

As already mentioned, you must make clear your trading identity and the means of communicating in writing with you. Any description of your goods and services must be fair and accurate, as in any advertising or promotional material. If your site gathers personal data from people visiting the site, you will have to comply with data protection law, as described below. If you include third-party material on your site, you must be sure not to infringe copyright, any other terms they have imposed or other rights they may have.

However, the nature of websites and the opportunity they provide for visitors to interact with them, contribute materials to them and, in some cases, purchase goods from them, opens up many more issues of liability, exposure and protection. Again, we would suggest you take expert advice based on your specific situation, but essentially you need to impose terms that limit your liability to claims against you, limit what visitors may do with material on your site and, if appropriate, what they may contribute. Most importantly, visitors must accept your terms before accessing the site. This is the electronic version of their formally accepting your terms and conditions in a contract.

Credit control

As a former business mentor never tired of telling us, 'You haven't made a sale until the money's in the bank'. If you have come from corporate life, you may think every transaction has to be on 30-day terms. Wrong! Payment terms are whatever the parties agree, from 'cash with order' through all the variations to 'net cash 180 days' (which we don't recommend).

From the seller's point of view, payment in advance is perfect, but you must then deliver the product or service strictly in accordance with the contract. If payment follows the delivery, even if it's just a few days after, you are into the realms of credit and must ensure you get your money according to the terms of the contract.

If your business falls into this category, and the majority do, we strongly advise you check out the buyer's credit record and their ability to pay, even if you are convinced they are 'OK'. You may be surprised at what you find, but it is better to find out before, when you can change the way you do business with them, rather than after, when you're playing catch-up with someone who is less honourable or in more difficulty than you thought!

It is rare to resort to the courts to recover a debt, but it is reassuring to know that the option is there if you need it. In fact, a solicitor's letter may be all it takes, because very few people want the stigma of a CCJ (County Court Judgment) in their record, even if it's been discharged.

We would just say that if payment is late, take immediate steps to recover it and chase it until you get it. You do not want to get a reputation for letting bad debts accumulate. Unfortunately, this is one of the more distasteful realities of small-business life, but it really is worth organising to ensure you get your money promptly. There are plenty of reasonably priced (and legal) options for both running credit checks and collecting money, leaving you free to run the business and focus on the more positive aspects of human nature!

3. Recruitment and employment

One reason many small businesses do everything they can not to employ staff is the raft of regulations associated with it, which they view as getting more and more complicated.

However, there are few businesses that can grow very much without employing staff, and it is really essential to do things properly and legally to ensure you are not exposed to claims of unfair or illegal practices at any stage. Once you are aware of your basic obligations and have systems in place, it is not difficult to comply. In fact, it makes life a lot easier for all concerned.

We strongly recommend that you consult a qualified HR practitioner or employment lawyer to discuss your specific situation, but some basic rules are:

- Have written employment contracts. These set out the terms of employment and legally must include details of their place of work, pay, hours of work, holiday entitlement, sickness arrangements and notice of termination. Bear in mind that the notice period does not go both ways; broadly speaking, you have to give 1 week's notice for every full year of service they have completed, to a maximum of 12 weeks, but their notice to you is 1 week, although you can agree a longer time period. There are some variations on this, so advice is necessary!

  It is then best practice to incorporate the job description, which defines the employee's job, tasks and activities and their level of responsibility. An employee should have their contract within 2 months of starting their employment.

- Have written policies and an employee handbook. Ensure every employee has access to a copy and they have acknowledged that in writing. Your policies and the handbook will set out what employees can expect from you and what you expect from them in terms of performance and behaviour, and especially the detailed grievance and disciplinary procedures.

- Have, and fully understand, an equal opportunity (EO) policy. These days, equal opportunity, or its mirror image non-discrimination, covers gender, race, ethnic origin, religion, sexual orientation, disability and age. The wording of job advertisements and selection criteria and the language used in interviews can be a minefield for the unwary, so take advice from an experienced practitioner. Note also that EO regulations apply even if you decide not to employ someone, if it can be shown that during the process you have contravened any of the regulations.

- Have a formal grievance procedure that allows employees to air their dissatisfaction or concerns without recrimination, and ensure it is followed to the letter.

- Have a formal disciplinary procedure that gives employees the opportunity to correct behaviour or improve performance, but also makes clear what activities or behaviour will lead to dismissal. The procedure must require that interactions with employees are documented and communicated.

If these basics are in place and you can demonstrate that you are following them to the letter, you will be in a strong position to defend any claims against you. However, employment legislation is changing all the time, so it is vital to keep up to date or maintain the means to do so.

Health and safety

Health and safety is a significant element within employment law, but you also have obligations to everyone affected by your activities, not just to your staff, and it is therefore best looked at separately. At this point, please resist the temptation to roll your eyes; much H&S law is sensible, reasonable and straightforward to follow, once you have complied with the basics. Even if you do not employ staff but, for example, have associates who may work on your premises, you still have some basic obligations.

If you employ anyone, even part-time, you must:

- Have current employers liability insurance.

- Appoint a named person competent to help you meet your H&S responsibilities; this can be you, a staff member or an independent practitioner.

- Have a H&S Policy that sets out how you manage health and safety in your business. This will include how you assess and control the risks to health and safety and how you will respond to an accident.

It is best if the policy is short and easily memorised by both you and your employees, because it governs everyone's behaviour and choices when they are at work.

- Provide a safe and healthy environment, with hazards identified and risks controlled to an acceptable level. Your premises must be safe and hygienic, with toilets, washing facilities and drinking water.

- Assess the risk of fire and put a variety of countermeasures in place based on the assessment to minimise the risk and to enable all employees to escape in the event of fire.

- Ensure that everyone working on your site (i.e. employees, contractors or associates) understands and complies with your policy and safety rules (they also have an equivalent legal responsibility to comply with your policy and rules and to help you as required to discharge your responsibility).

- Consult your employees to develop safe systems of work that permit hazardous operations to be conducted safely, efficiently and successfully.

- Require all accidents and the actions taken as a result to be recorded in a log or book.

- Understand the regulations and procedure for reporting safety-related incidents.

The Health and Safety Executive (HSE) website provides excellent guidance for small businesses, designed to keep people safe and healthy while not placing too great a burden on them.

Data protection

This is governed by the Data Protection Act (DPA) and is not an issue just for big companies!

If you hold personal data for any reason, such as to comply with legal employment and taxation requirements, you must adhere to some basic principles. This can become complex as personal data can be held in a bewildering number of places, so we recommend that you check out your specific circumstances with a DPA expert.

In essence, the acquisition, use and processing of personal data must be:

- for specific, defined purposes
- at a level appropriate to the need
- accurate and up to date
- destroyed when no longer needed
- secure

Summary

There is a large body of law that governs how we do business and how we treat people in the course of doing business. We must be aware of our obligations while at the same time acknowledging that it provides us with certain valuable protections.

Business Continuity

We have already addressed a number of issues in this chapter (see pages 123–127) about protecting your IT system from catastrophic failure.

However, other disasters can strike that can also plunge a business into crisis in a flash. No one likes to dwell on them, but it is worth spending a little time to reflect on what could happen that could cause your business to crash and burn. You can then think what you might do, firstly to minimise the likelihood of its happening and secondly to recover from it, should the worst happen despite your best efforts.

In some businesses and organisations this is called crisis management. This is dramatic and certainly catches your attention, but we prefer the less abrasive and more optimistic term business continuity to ensure we focus on the escape route, not the crisis.

The following potentially catastrophic events all happened in the past 5 years to business owners we know or have met:

- Their office/factory was destroyed by fire.

- They had a serious accident a) on the motorway returning from a client and b) on holiday.

- They contracted a serious illness.

- An employee was seriously injured in an accident on their premises.

- A major client went under, owing a sum equivalent to 25% of their turnover.

- A major client sued them for £1 million for giving bad advice.

- A business partner/a senior member of staff absconded with the contents of the bank account.

- The taxman did a detailed investigation of their business tax affairs.

Thinking of your own circumstances, consider what the impact would be on you and your business if these happened to you, and what measures you would put in place to:

- minimise the chances of its happening

- protect yourself and your income if it did happen

- enable the business to recover and continue

Clearly, the answers will be rather different if your business is a two-person consultancy or a manufacturing company employing 20 people, but one common protection for most of these risks is insurance. You must have employer liability insurance if you employ anybody, and anyone in a consultative profession ought to have professional indemnity insurance. To understand in depth what you can insure and under what terms, it is best to consult a commercial insurance broker.

Your attitude to business continuity will also influence the decision of any lender you approach for a loan. This is discussed in more depth in Chapter 5 (see pages 178–184).

– Chapter 4 –
Managing Yourself

Chapter 4 – Managing Yourself

This chapter examines how you, your actions and your habits and behaviours can affect the performance of the business, and what you can do to overcome those things that limit you and nurture those that promote the growth of the business.

Contents of Chapter 4:

- **Attitude and mindset** – if you don't believe in yourself and the business, no one else will.

- **Time management and getting organised** – creating the space to focus on what is important and doing it in the most efficient way possible.

- **Delegation and managing staff** – knowing when to let go and let them do their jobs, so you can do yours.

- **Management meetings** – making sure these are effective review and decision-making meetings.

- **Coaching and professional development** – being open to new ideas and making time to improve your own performance.

- **Taking care of yourself** – if you don't, no one else will!

Attitude and Mindset

"If you think you can or you think you can't, you're probably right." –
Henry Ford

People set up and run their own businesses for all sorts of reasons. The
UK is blessed in that it is very easy, quick and inexpensive to set up in
business compared to many of our continental neighbours, where the
concept of entrepreneurship is regarded rather differently (despite the fact
that 'entrepreneur' is a French word!).

We assume that you have a passion for what you do, or at the very least
you thoroughly enjoy and relish the challenge of running your own
business. We will understand if some of the difficulties, setbacks and
challenges have dented your confidence, but underneath you know that
there is a way to overcome them and to become successful.

In fact, this is absolutely critical to the success of your business. You
must have cast-iron belief in that, because this will shape your attitude to
organising your business life and especially to how other people perceive
you. In a nutshell, if they sense that you do not believe in yourself, they
will not believe in you either and they will avoid you. Your lack of self-
belief will rapidly become a self-fulfilling prophecy.

Self-confidence should not be confused with arrogance. Self-confidence
implies a degree of self-knowledge and accepts there are certain things
that still need to be learnt or are better left to others. If people feel they
are dealing with someone who is always right and does not respect
other people's opinions and abilities, it will put a serious brake on the
relationship.

We have met and assisted many business owners whose belief and
attitude needed to be realigned before they could make progress.

*Mary was a highly competent bookkeeper, but her self-confidence when
we first met was close to zero. She could not believe that others would
value what she did and consequently set her sights very low. As a result,
her business was 'pants' (to use one of her favourite technical terms).
When we explored what she could really do and she overcame her terror*

of networking (which took 5 minutes at the first event we took her to),
her network of key contacts mushroomed and her business blossomed.

The fundamental point was that by restoring her self-belief, her attitude changed to a positive 'can-do' and it started to shine through in her interactions with staff, networking contacts, prospects and clients, who all responded in kind. This further boosted her confidence and enabled her to acquire and apply the knowledge to tackle the actions that would grow her business.

Time Management and Getting Organised

As we have observed in several parts of the book already, the owners of small businesses often have to wear several hats as they perform many different functions necessary to running a business. While managers in larger organisations assign people to do these various things, the business owner has to assign time and cannot do everything at once.

Managing your time well and getting properly organised are basic skills that all business owners must acquire, both for the sake of the business and for their own sanity.

Time management is very much an individual thing. Some people seem to have time to do everything they need to do, while others are always trying to catch up, leaving important things to the last minute. Most people are somewhere in-between, but just about everyone agrees that they would benefit from managing their time better.

There are many reasons why people manage their time badly, and equally as many tips we can suggest to help. You may find it useful to group these ideas into three categories, as follows:

1. **Prioritise** – Are you doing too much? In which case, prioritise tasks by importance and urgency, and push all the unimportant tasks to the bottom of the pile. If they don't get done, so what?

2. **Get organised** – Are your workplace and task list well organised and do you work efficiently? If not, reorganise so you can find

things when you need them, focus on the tasks that need your full attention and ensure that similar tasks are done in batches rather than in 'dribs and drabs'.

3. **Minimise distraction** – Organise your tasks and your day to suit your working style and educate your staff and clients about when you are available for them and when you are not. This lets you concentrate for the time spans that suit you and establish a working discipline that either removes sources of distraction altogether or allows you to ignore them until you are ready to deal with them (phone calls, email etc.).

Prioritise

This is perhaps the quickest of quick wins!

List all the routine tasks you do and allocate them into four categories; as new tasks descend on you, allocate them immediately into one of these four categories:

- Important and urgent (the IUs)

- Important but not urgent (the INUs)

- Unimportant and urgent (the UUs)

- Unimportant and not urgent (the UNUs)

It's immediately clear what you should be focusing on! If it's hard to decide on importance, ask yourself "What's the worst that can happen if I don't do this?" It's surprising how everything seems important until you turn the spotlight on it!

You will also notice the INU category; it is really critical to carve out time in the day or week to do these things, otherwise the clamour of everyday life crowds them out and they either do not get done at all or you are rushing to do them at the last minute, with the inevitable stress to yourself and the increased likelihood of mistakes and other marks of poor quality, not to mention the other urgent important things that get elbowed aside.

They are often projects and reports with a deadline of sometime in the future, but many of them are continuous tasks such as following up sales calls. We strongly recommend that you enter a regular block of time in your diary and treat it as an unbreakable appointment, so other things do not encroach on that time.

Get organised

Now that your tasks are prioritised, you can turn your attention to the mountain of paperwork on your desk, so you're left with just what's important and can see if you can do it more efficiently.

The 4 Ds

The majority of tasks are accompanied by paperwork, usually too much of it until you need a vital piece of paper and can't find it. If you find it difficult to get work done because your desk looks like it has been the venue for a rats' picnic, you could be suffering from 'desk stress'. Here are some practical ways to control paperwork before it overwhelms you and to reinforce the prioritising you have done. But first, you may enjoy this simple quiz to assess your level of 'desk stress':

1. Are there ten or more items on my desk right now?

2. Are there more than three files or projects on my desk right now?

3. Does my desk have an in-basket?

4. Do I put my desk work into separate piles?

5. In the last week, have I had trouble finding something on my desk?

6. Do other people think twice before putting something on my desk?

7. Is there a pile of unread work within sight on my desk right now?

8. Am I known for a messy desk?

9. Can other people find things on my desk?

10. Do I try to clear my desk every night?

Score one point for each 'yes' answer.

7–10: you would be in intensive care if desk stress was a medical condition. Your messy desk is hampering your productivity and could be affecting how others see you.

5–6: you may still be a desk stress candidate who is wasting valuable time and energy because of your messy desk. You must get organised and take control of your working environment.

1–4: you appear not to be suffering from desk stress, but you should make sure you keep on top of the stream of notes, papers, messages and reading matter, so that it doesn't build up and drown you.

Wherever you found yourself on this 1–10 scale, you may benefit from the '4D' technique to sort out your paperwork and reflect the prioritising you have now done:

Allocate each piece of paper to one of four piles. Resist the temptation to create a fifth 'don't know – can't decide' pile. There is no D5 in 4D!

- D1   Destroy it

- D2   Delegate it

- D3   Decide when you are going to do it

- D4   Do it now

D1 is the easiest. This pile corresponds to the UUs and UNUs above. Take a moment to enjoy the feeling of halving your paperwork as the pile lands in the recycling bin.

D2 may take some thought and some planning or training, but can someone else do it instead of you? You should be aiming to get to the point where you are focusing on doing what only you can do. Think laterally here; delegation may mean outsourcing or even automating a task or process, so that you do not have to spend your precious time on it.

The VAT specialist we mentioned in chapter 2 (page 28) doubled the time he could spend on the section of his process that needed his unique knowledge and skills. There were several other relatively simple steps in the process that he was able to standardise and train an assistant to do without his constant supervision.

D3 is perhaps the most crucial; these will be the INUs that require your skill and knowledge and cannot be delegated. Tasks like writing a detailed report or completing a public sector tender need time assigned in your diary so that they will be completed in good time and can be checked to ensure they are as good as they can be. Regular tasks like following up sales calls need to be allocated blocks of time to ensure they happen.

This really defines your overall approach to your job; by getting organised you can be focused and calm, work to a high standard and complete every important task on time, without being chased by anxious clients or your own conscience!

Finally, D4. You are now left with the IUs. These will be obvious, so dig in and work on clearing them.

These days, desk stress has been joined by its electronic cousin, email overload, and much the same can be said of the electronic desk as the real one. The platform may be different, but the principle is the same: keep what you need in order to get important work done and ditch or distribute the rest.

Group regular tasks into batches

As a small business, you or one of your staff may be involved in frequent regular routine tasks and, in the interests of keeping them under control, do them as soon as they arise. It could be helpful to ask yourself: "If I only did this once a week, would it matter to the business?" If the answer is no, then ask yourself the follow-up question "If I only did this once a week, how much time would it save?"

> *One of our clients used to invoice their clients as soon as the task was done, which on the face of it was good practice. The result was that, on average, once per day they opened up the computer program to create the invoice, printed off two copies, put the top copy into an envelope, addressed and stamped it and put the file copy into a ring binder. Each time, it took at least 20 minutes, which meant they were spending up to 2 hours a week on invoicing. We got them to do the invoicing once a*

week and they did all five together in only 30 minutes, saving over an
hour per week!

You may like to have a look at your lists and see what you can condense
from daily to weekly and weekly to monthly.

Create a default diary

A default diary establishes the pattern of your week and month, within
which you slot in specific appointments and tasks. So for example,
you assign the first half hour of the day and the first half hour in the
afternoon to dealing with phone messages and email, and the last half
hour to planning and preparing for the following day. Tuesday and Friday
are your marketing days (networking events, following up referrals,
replying to LinkedIn invitations, commenting in online discussions etc.),
Monday is your office (INU) day and Wednesday and Thursday are your
sales appointment days.

Once you have prioritised new and incoming tasks, and ditched or
delegated some of them, you can slot the remainder into the appropriate
block of your default diary and, as time goes on, your staff and clients
will get to know broadly when you are available and when you are not.

3. Minimise distraction

Distraction comes in three distinct forms:

- Interruptions: these are telephones, emails, text messages and
  someone putting their head round the door (have you got a
  minute?) or asking you to do something outside your normal brief.

- Lack of concentration: this is an internal distraction that has
  your mind switching onto something else or just wandering off
  somewhere.

- Procrastination: this is the ability to put off to tomorrow what
  ought to be done today, despite every logical brain cell screaming
  NO!

Distraction really is the patron saint of time wasting and is the number one enemy of time management! You can prioritise your tasks and arrange to do them in the most efficient way, but if you keep putting them off or can't concentrate on getting them done, you're doomed!

Interruptions

It has been estimated that it can take between 5 and 20 minutes to restore the level of concentration you had before an interruption. If you need to work uninterrupted, you can switch the phone to silent or 'do not disturb' and ignore emails or texts when they 'ping' (in fact, turn off the sound alert altogether). However, always respond to these messages as soon as the period is over, otherwise you will get a reputation for ignoring the very people you need and who need you.

More tricky are interruptions by people needing to talk to you. You need to assess politely but firmly if it can wait or must be dealt with immediately. It might be urgent or something that you can answer in 5 seconds that would take them 2 hours to solve, so you have to use your judgement. After a while, people will know that 'door open' means come in, 'door shut' means only come in if it truly can't wait.

People asking you for favours or to do things outside your normal scope, or even outside the block assigned to it in your default diary, can also be difficult to handle satisfactorily. It is perfectly acceptable to negotiate a different time or day, even if it's a client or prospect wanting to see you, but remember they have to manage their time as well so you may have to be flexible.

The ability to say no without causing offence is a really important skill to learn as a manager and business owner. If your instinct is telling you 'You really don't want to be doing this', you must find a way to say it.

Lack of concentration

You must first decide if this is a temporary issue arising from a real preoccupation with a serious problem, in which case you should either deal with the problem or block it out while you deal with the immediate task, or if it is a general characteristic.

To tackle this, you need to recognise your working style and be honest with yourself about your ability to concentrate:

- Do you work better in short bursts with frequent short breaks, or for hours without interruption?
- Once doing something, can you concentrate on it, blocking everything else out, or do you find your mind wandering?
- Can you plough on until it's finished and then review it, or do you find yourself pausing to admire what you've just done and 'micro-editing' it?

Two positive techniques might work for you: simple, good old-fashioned willpower and promising yourself a reward when you've finished.

If neither of these works, even when you are working in your optimum conditions, then you will have to resort to fear – fear of what could happen if you don't buckle down and get on with it. It's called 'lighting the fuse on the bomb'. There is nothing like a real deadline, with some drastic consequence if you miss it, to concentrate the mind!

Procrastination

This is the ability of the right-hand side of your brain, the creative side that deals with your emotions, to swamp out the left-hand side that deals with logic and analysis. It breezily says there's no problem putting off that boring task because the interesting stuff is, in fact, far more urgent, and completely muffles your left brain's protests.

Once again, it's a matter of being honest with yourself and recognising that you are prone to it. Deadlines, a little reward or short break on completing the most important tasks first or drawing up a list of the day's tasks with numbers assigned to them in the order that you need to do them are all possible techniques for dealing with procrastination.

However, the right brain does have a weakness that you can exploit. Usually, the tasks you put off are the ones you don't enjoy or the ones you are not looking forward to, like the phone call to an angry client or confronting a wayward employee. This is your emotions trying to shield you from unpleasantness or boredom.

This is a real killer for business owners! You just know it's going to eat away at you, ruining your day. Finally, when your left brain insists that you buckle down and do it, guess what? It wasn't that bad after all.

So when deciding on the order in which to do things, make the worst task, the one you are least looking forward to, the **very first thing you do**, and get it out of the way. Mark Twain called it 'eating a frog for breakfast'!

Delegation and Managing Staff

We looked at the whole HR question in Chapter 3 (see pages 106–114) and also touched on HR issues in Chapter 2 (see pages 77–78) when discussing the resources you need to deliver your product or service.

This section looks at it from your point of view and, in particular, the difficulty business owners can have in letting go and trusting others to do a good job without looking over their shoulder all the time.

We saw in the last section that delegation can be a really effective way to free up your time to do the things that only you are qualified to do, so it makes absolutely no sense to continue doing what you have engaged someone else to do, nor to waste time checking every 5 minutes that they are doing it right.

This is not to say that you should tolerate inferior work, and certainly not that you should do it again yourself to put it right, although in an extreme circumstance you may have to do that to get the order ready for a customer.

It can be a major transition from doing everything yourself to engaging someone else to help, especially if the tasks that you need to delegate are ones you actually like doing.

The only way to deal with this issue is firstly, to acknowledge your own feelings and fears about it and secondly, to plan how you are going to organise things so that you can trust another person to take over some of your precious work and do it to the standard the business requires.

Once again, we can be dealing with a conflict between your right brain (emotions) and left brain (logic). Your right brain is worried about losing part of yourself; diverting time you need to fulfil orders to finding someone who is half-way decent and training them; and finding their work is shoddy and having to do it again. These are real fears and need to be taken seriously.

In fact, they are really useful because they point to the important things you need to do to get the right person in place, to ensure they know exactly what the job requires and what standard is expected of them and to feel they can ask you if they are not sure of something. In the early days you will, of course, be checking their work and coaching them to do it the way you want it done, but your aim is to let them get on with it so you can get on with running the business.

This approach is your left brain calming your right brain by presenting a solution to all its immediate fears and showing that in the long run it will make all sorts of things better. Once the right brain has gone away feeling much happier, the left brain turns back to Chapter 3 (see pages 106–114) and sets about the process of finding the right person, getting them up to speed as quickly as possible and developing them to become real contributors to the business.

Management Meetings

You may have left corporate life, mightily relieved that you would never again have to suffer those interminable meetings that went nowhere and achieved nothing.

Badly run meetings are the bane of working life, but when they are well organised and well run, they are a highly effective mechanism to communicate, impart information and make decisions. This is just as important in a small business as in a corporation.

Every business should review its progress regularly and make decisions on what it will do next, whether it's short term (the next month) or long term (next year). The monthly management meeting is the best medium for the routine running of the business, and an annual meeting for reviewing the previous year and planning the next one.

Even a one-person business should take the time to review their business once a month and plan the following month. If there are two people or more in the business, it takes a meeting!

As we said at length earlier in this chapter (see pages 148–156), time is precious and needs to be managed effectively, so taking time out for a meeting had better be worth it!

Let us assume that you are in charge of the meeting, even if you have a partner with whom you run the business on equal terms:

- First of all, decide if you need to meet in person or can conduct the meeting over the phone or in a conference call.

- Ensure people know the meeting rules and etiquette, especially in a phone or internet conference; for example, if two people speak at the same time, their voices cancel each other out and no one can hear anything!

- Prepare an agenda, giving details of the topics and timings, as well as the purpose of the meeting and what the outcome should be. Generally, it will be to review progress, discuss issues, impart information and make decisions. It is **not** a problem-solving forum!

- Distribute the agenda in time to let people know what they have to prepare. Have a 'default agenda' so that topics such as finance, sales, marketing and delivery are there every month, with other topics added as appropriate.

- Make people responsible for preparing their updates and circulating them beforehand, and make sure everyone else has studied them, so the meeting can focus on discussing the content, raising any issues and making decisions.

- Ensure the meeting starts and finishes on time, with any required decisions made. Do not wait for latecomers and do not brief them on what's already happened when they finally arrive. They will soon get the message.

- If a subject starts to take up too much time or begins to become a problem-solving session, bring it to a halt and arrange to continue it outside the meeting with only the people who need to be there.

- Distribute the minutes within 24 hours if possible.

- If you yourself are going to be late for someone else's meeting, phone ahead to let them know so they can decide whether to wait for you or not.

Coaching and Professional Development

It is very easy when you are run off your feet in the heat of battle to feel there is no time or mental energy left to expose yourself to new ideas or learn how other people are dealing with the same problems you are.

" Tell him we haven't got time for any of his bright ideas — we've got a battle on our hands "

Some professions that require qualifications provide and insist on continuous development to keep up with current trends and ensure people stay up to date.

Sadly, running a business does not come in that category, so you will have to organise and make time for your own development.

It need not take as much time as you imagine. Many networking and business development groups incorporate some training and learning in their regular meetings, delivered by fellow members or specialists in particular topics. For many business owners, this is the only professional development they get and can be an additional and highly valuable element in their membership package.

However, you may decide that this is not really enough. Good as they may be, regular professional development slots in what are primarily marketing meetings can only go so far. There are two possibilities you may like to consider: masterminding and individual coaching.

Masterminding

A 'mastermind' group is a self-help group consisting of five or six like-minded people with broadly equivalent experience and positions in their organisations, meeting every 1–2 months. Unlike their personas in the outside world, they are completely frank with each other about their problems, fears and anxieties. Someone in the group has probably encountered and maybe solved a similar problem before, and the others chip in with their thoughts and ideas about it. They understand your business but are detached from it, so they can see it from your target market's point of view and can think objectively about it. They can provide you with suggestions and be a sounding board for your own ideas. This can help you over that sticking point or nutty problem, but perhaps its most profound influence is summed up in the saying 'A problem shared is a problem halved'. You can feel lonely and exposed when owning and running a business, and it can be very comforting to know that you can turn to half a dozen people who know you and your business, and whom you respect and trust wholeheartedly.

A really effective mastermind group has some key characteristics that are worth noting:

- The members like and trust each other and have broadly similar experience and positions in their organisations.

- They understand and take a great interest in each other's businesses and do all they can to help and support each other.

- They are not suppliers or clients of each other, nor members of the same organisation. This prevents any conflict of interest or other reason that could inhibit them from speaking openly and freely with each other.

- They meet regularly.

- They treat meeting with each other as if they were meeting with a major client.

- After each member has outlined a problem and received ideas and suggestions from the others, they commit to implementing at least one and report back at the next meeting. This is perhaps the only time the owner is held accountable to another person or group, and it is the real 'acid test' of the effectiveness of the group (otherwise it is just another talking shop).

Business coaching

Have you noticed how serious sportsmen and women always have a performance coach to help them improve further, when we already think they are brilliant at what they do?

If you really want to make progress and improve your performance in running your business, you may want to consider working with a business, or executive, coach.

Firstly, let us be clear that business coaching is not business advice! Advice in the end is only advice: you are not obliged to do or commit to anything. Coaching is quite different: it is a mutual commitment on the part of both you and the coach to do new things, or to do existing things differently, to improve your overall performance. In business coaching, as in sports coaching, action, commitment and accountability are all necessary elements of this process, with you and the coach each playing a specific, defined role.

It starts with you deciding that you want and need help.

The coach's role is to find out what you want to achieve, analyse what you are currently doing, decide what you need to do differently and help you do it. This can be demonstrating different techniques, introducing new ideas, bringing in a specialist or simply holding you to account for getting things done; most likely it will be a combination of some or all these things.

Your role now is to accept the coach's analysis and to **work very hard** at putting the coach's ideas and instructions into action. The coach's role continues by holding you to account for getting things done and making life very uncomfortable for you if you don't!

Recruiting a coach

You are recruiting, in effect, an important and probably expensive member of staff, so you need to ensure you get the right person in terms of both their credibility and track record and your ability to respect and get on with each other. In this very individual field, personal referral from someone whose opinion you respect and value is probably the best way to go about it.

Be aware that a good coach will not take you on unless they are convinced that you are serious, and that means being prepared and able to pay the price as well as being committed to the programme.

Cost

Having mentioned it, we should comment on cost and value.

Business coaching is an unregulated profession; anyone can set up in business and call themselves a coach. You therefore have no professional standards or qualifications to reassure you, only what they tell you and, perhaps most importantly, what other people tell you. A business coach who has developed a good track record, and has other successful people recommending them, will not come cheap, and neither should they.

Therefore, like any investment in business, you must judge the outlay on coaching by the expected and required return. You have to give it time to work, but after a while, if you are not satisfied, you must call a halt and try something or someone else.

Taking Care of Yourself

If you have read the section in Chapter 3 (see pages 143–144) on business continuity, you may have considered the impact on your business if you were to become seriously ill or were badly hurt in an accident, and been sufficiently sobered by the thought that you went further and started to think of ways to minimise the chance of these things happening.

This section looks at this issue in more detail for the day-to-day good of both the business and you and to ward off the extreme case where you are incapacitated for months.

It is worth bearing in mind that persistent tiredness or feeling 'under the weather' may be a symptom of something more serious or can lead to something more serious. Likewise, a minor accident may have at its root something that on another occasion, and with a dose of bad luck, could cause major injury. You must therefore regard these apparently trivial events as warnings and act on whatever lessons you draw from them.

Health and well-being

The human body is a wonderful machine, but like all machines it needs care, maintenance and the occasional stay in the garage to operate at its best. Illness, fatigue and stress all take their toll on the body and need to be taken seriously if we are to work to our full potential.

Illness

Most of us enjoy good health most of the time, suffering occasional 'minor' complaints like coughs and colds, but generally recovering with, at worst, a couple of days off and some over-the-counter medicine. We are not at our best, but somehow manage to keep going and struggle through, with no significant or lasting impact on the business.

At least, we think not. By 'struggling through', we may not be giving our body the time and rest it needs to deal with the problem. Virus infections, in particular, can be very persistent, leaving us fatigued and operating at well below par for ages and making us more vulnerable to picking up something else. Who knows what mistakes we make or opportunities we miss when half the body's energy is taken up fighting the battle within?

The advice 'if symptoms persist, see your doctor' should be taken seriously!

> *Men, and especially macho men, are their own worst enemy in this respect. Some years ago, a good business friend, a charming, charismatic but rather macho character, was too busy to ask his doctor about a persistent pain in his stomach. He put it down to indigestion from his busy business life. He finally found out what it was, but what may have been a treatable cancer was by now too advanced. He was dead within two months.*

Fatigue

Running a business can be exhausting; physically, with the long hours and long-distance travel, and mentally, with the pressures of getting business, dealing with clients and staff and keeping the finances straight. Many business owners admit they don't get enough sleep, either working till late or waking too early with their minds already racing.

If this is the case, there may be things you can do yourself to reduce your workload (so you do not have to work late) or calm your mind, and both are to do with managing your time, getting organised and taking breaks. If you have not read the earlier section in this chapter on time management and getting organised (see pages 148–156), now would be a good time to do so.

If your day involves a lot of repetitive tasks or tasks you do not enjoy, even if they are not physically demanding, boredom has a depressing effect on the system that feels just like tiredness and is the exact opposite of excitement and stimulation, when all feelings of sluggishness vanish! If this is your business life, break up the day and insert some enjoyable or exciting tasks, or at the very least a little reward for having got through the last hour.

It is important, when much of our business life is spent sitting at a computer or driving a car, to take regular exercise. This not only loosens the muscles that imperceptibly tighten up when we are sitting for long periods, but relaxes the mind after periods of concentration and stimulates the circulation to increase the blood flow to the brain and the other vital organs.

We do not talk about 'recharging our batteries' for nothing. During the day, we place huge demands on our minds and bodies and they need to recharge overnight while we are sleeping and there is minimal demand on them. This is also thought to be the time when the mind rests but is still active, processing and organising all the inputs from the day and making some sense of them. Waking up early with your mind racing could be a symptom that it can't cope!

In addition, by continuously placing extremely high demands on the body and not allowing it to fully recharge, it is possible to develop a more chronic fatigue ('running on empty') and the need for a longer recharge, such as a 'flop and drop' holiday.

Breaks in the working day are effectively short recharging periods and really help to get you through the day, especially if you are not moving around. Studies have shown that the morning and afternoon tea and coffee breaks really do increase productivity, so do not allow just your staff to take them, take them yourself! Similarly, allow yourself a proper lunch break of at least 45–60 minutes and get away from your desk.

Being able to 'switch off' and relax the mind and body is another essential skill for business owners. If you have trouble doing this or the suggestions above do not improve matters, seek help, and preferably not from legal or illegal substances!

Stress

Stress can also be both a cause and an effect. It is the result of pressure that we can't handle or control. The mind racing in the early hours is a typical symptom of it.

A stressed body or mind consumes far more energy than normal, making an already bad situation worse as you have even less energy to deal with the pressures of business and life than usual. If you don't get to the bottom of what is causing you to be stressed and deal with it – and that is never as easy as it sounds – you can become ill and you can be forced to take extended time off to recover. In the extreme case, you may have to change your lifestyle altogether.

You can do various physical and mental exercises to relieve the symptoms of stress and give you more energy to deal with life, but it is far better to deal with the root cause, if possible.

Meanwhile, find something to make you laugh, and the more uncontrollably you can laugh the better!

Anger

A common cause of stress is anger, or rather the inability to handle it effectively. Anger is a natural emotional response when something of importance or value to us is threatened or challenged. It can be constructive if it forces us to act to deal with the issue, or it can be destructive if our actions cause harm to ourselves or others. That harm can be physical, mental or emotional, and can occur at once or sometime in the future.

Most of the time we deal with such occurrences and move on; a muttered expletive or a stamp of the foot is enough to relieve the tension. But occasionally we can be overwhelmed by the emotion and lose control, and this is when it can get serious and potentially dangerous.

We are once again back to left brain (logic) and right brain (emotion). The key here is to re-engage the left brain as quickly as possible to regain control and defuse the situation, whether you are angry yourself or confronted by someone else's anger. Usually, in business, you can empathise with an angry person without agreeing with them or conceding anything, and this is the first step to calming them and helping them to talk through the issue.

It can be easy to think we have dealt with issues when, in fact, we have simply bottled them up, when they can fester, build and cause untold mental and emotional stress. Running your own business is challenging enough without these unwelcome distractions. In such a case, it is truly worthwhile to have someone to confide in, who can empathise and help you take hold of the issue and deal with it.

Safety

If you have premises and staff, you will be familiar with the steps you must take to keep them safe. We discussed them at length in the HR and legal sections in Chapter 3 (see pages 106–114 and 133–143).

However, it is easy to overlook the fact that your own safety is just as important and needs at least as much attention, given your responsibilities and pressures. We strongly recommend that you take a little time to think about your working day and working environment and identify the hazards that lurk round every corner. Some will be external, inherent in the environment around you, and some will be internal, arising from your own behaviour and attitude to risk. External hazards can be permanent (a beam sticking out at head height) or temporary (an icy pavement). Some days you are calm and patient, always using the pedestrian crossing; other days you are tired, flustered or in a hurry and take whatever shortcuts you can.

The hazards that you are most likely to face are in the office (trips and falls, strains from lifting awkward loads, problems from sitting badly for a long time) and in the car, especially driving when tired or stressed.

Ultimately, how you behave and what risks you take are your choice. Give some thought to your responsibilities, especially the people at work and at home who rely on you, and then make your choice.

Now make a conscious decision that you will always make that choice, whatever the circumstances. Not only will you give yourself the best chance to remain uninjured, but you will set the right example to your people and have the moral authority to insist that they operate to your standards.

– Chapter 5 –
The Growth Plan

Chapter 5 – The Growth Plan

After much analysis and soul-searching, you are now ready to put your plan together.

Up to this point, the chapters have been about analysis and reflection of your current position. All along, you will have had ideas of things to change or do differently and new things to do that will move the business along. Hopefully, you have been making a note of those things as you thought of them, because you almost certainly will not remember them all now that you need them!

Before charging straight into the plan, it is important to take stock of all the key areas of the business to ensure you have identified the strengths that need to be protected and nurtured, and the weak points that could derail the business and prevent you achieving your goal.

There are, therefore, two fundamental actions to make sure your plan is effective:

1. Write it down

2. Review it regularly

A written plan is said to be ten times more likely to be put into practice than one that exists only in your head. Putting it down on paper is a powerful way of embedding it in your consciousness and giving you a template for action that sometime down the road will remind and reassure you that you are on the right track. It is also a wonderful way to convince your lieutenants and staff that you have a vision and a plan for the future of the company and that you want them to be part of it.

The regular review is what really keeps it alive. We suggest that you devote a half-day every 3 months to reviewing your progress and deciding the specific actions for the next 3 months.

Many plans reveal the need for a sizeable injection of cash to fund the growth strategy at some point in the future, so we have included some helpful comments on preparing the ground before you approach potential lenders for finance.

This chapter consists of:

- **Evaluation (SWOT analysis)**
- **Writing and reviewing the plan**
- **Financing your growth**

Evaluation (SWOT Analysis)

The evaluation phase is best done in two parts. Firstly, we suggest you sum up the key elements of your business that match the sections in the book that are relevant to you. These should include:

- Your goal and milestones
- Your objectives, potential constraints and countermeasures
- Your products and services, target market, competition and USP
- Your current sales and marketing strategies
- Your current resources and administrative systems
- Your current financial position
- Your recent sales history and current order book

Secondly, you should draw a simple SWOT matrix. This is a very useful tool to highlight the key areas that need attention as you build up your plan.

SWOT stands for strengths, weaknesses, opportunities and threats. S and W are inside the business, O and T are outside the business. You put a tick to represent strengths and opportunities and a cross to represent weaknesses or threats. It should be no more than one A4 page at the most. We are not looking for a research thesis here.

It is always good to recognise your strengths first; this helps you to brace yourself for what follows, which will very likely be activities that are outside your comfort zone. To illustrate the power of a SWOT analysis in action, we offer two examples below, one in which the company's marketplace was about to change radically in the way it awarded contracts, the other in which the company's own approach was holding it back.

They illustrate very different strategies, but both examples show how to use the SWOT analysis so that the growth plan focuses on what needs to happen and the order it needs to happen in, right from the beginning.

Example 1 is a company that delivered sport and recreational services to schools, but the marketplace dynamics were about to change and leave them stranded.

SWOT Analysis 1

	Executive	Finance & Admin	Marketing & Sales	Delivery
Strengths				✓
Weaknesses	✗	✗	✗	
Opportunities	✓		✓	
Threats		✗		

Up to now, the business has been generated at the same pace as the resources to deliver it, which suggests that the marketing, the financing and the assignment of delivery resources have been effective.

The issue now is that external circumstances are about to change radically and the marketing methods that succeeded in the past will not be effective in the future. The good thing is that the business owners have recognised this in time to do something about it.

All of this means that the business and financial management, the marketing and selling effort and the administration of resources must change to meet the new challenge and thrive on it.

The analysis has thrown up a number of lucrative opportunities outside the education sector, which will both spread the risk and diversify the marketplace, as well as provide continuous work during school holiday periods. This suggests that there needs to be an immediate concentrated marketing effort in these other sectors, while as far as possible maintaining the core business in the education sector by adapting the company's systems to the new circumstances.

Example 2 is a medium-size specialised manufacturing company with a very strong technical, product development and engineering base, but a poorly developed commercial approach. The highly experienced production manager had recently been promoted by the board to manage the business, which by his own admission was well outside his comfort zone. At the outset, it was established that the business had to grow substantially – to double its turnover, in fact – to survive and prosper.

SWOT Analysis 2

	Executive	Finance & Admin	Marketing & Sales	Delivery
Strengths	✓			✓
Weaknesses		✗	✗	
Opportunities			✓	
Threats			✗	

Fortunately, the area that needs urgent attention – marketing – is the same as the area that presents the biggest opportunity, meaning that the solution will both solve the problem and realise the opportunity.

Manufacturing and customer service is very strong; indeed, it is the very essence of the company. However, the growth plan is going to place extra demands on production as well as on the newly promoted MD. It would therefore seem like a good idea to appoint an operations manager to oversee all aspects of production.

The executive branch is strong: the MD has the backing of the Chairman, the CEO and the shareholders. He has recognised that he must manage the whole business, not just the plant. This means stepping back and letting the production teams run manufacturing and increasing the marketing activity substantially to achieve the required growth.

Financially, the company is more stable than it was, but after several years of relatively flat performance, it is still only just about breaking even, which makes it vulnerable to a shock event such as the loss of a major client. The shareholders have been patient and generous up to now, but their expectation has been raised by the prospect of real growth and some return on their investment in the foreseeable future.

There are clearly many opportunities to capitalise on the company's technical and manufacturing expertise in this specialised field, but it will need some focused and carefully targeted marketing to find them and bring the company to their attention. Once this happens, there is little doubt that enough prospects will become profitable, sustainable clients, but the 'gestation period' is generally long, so the marketing effort must start immediately!

Growth is likely to come more or less equally from existing clients and new prospects, some of which will probably be overseas. Two parallel strategies will therefore be needed:

- a sales strategy aimed at existing clients and current prospects
- a marketing strategy to generate new prospects

In all cases, it will be vital to focus on 'jam today' to fill up the spare capacity and resist the temptation to tackle intellectually stimulating development that may take years to deliver a return, if at all. This means that new products may be investigated, but only if they can be produced in the current facilities and with the existing equipment, and there is an immediate demand for them.

In short, the growth strategy must deliver with little or no capital investment in new equipment, and must not work on products or markets either requiring substantial development or where there will be no demand until sometime in the future.

Writing and Reviewing the Plan

Writing the plan

Having made such efforts to get this far, you certainly do not want a plan that is going to sit untouched in a drawer. It has to be your guidebook and map, readily accessible for you to consult at key points to ensure you are where you ought to be, as you plan the next stage of the journey.

Given that your plan will be referred to frequently and regularly, you will want to keep it, and yourself, focused and efficient. We suggest you design it to serve as both the agenda for and the minutes of your review meetings.

Here is one layout we have found to be effective:

- Cover page with title and date and the time and date of the next review meeting.

- Page 1: The goal and milestones.

- Page 2: The revenue in the quarter just gone, and revenue targets for the next 12 quarters corresponding to the revenue necessary to achieve the milestones and goal. This will be a table, with an extra column for the actual revenues as you progress and a column for any relevant comment.

- Page 3: One or two paragraphs on the current position, a sentence or two that summarises the focus for the next 90 days and up to six specific actions (no more) plus the person responsible for each action, if appropriate.

- Page 4: Progress on actions from the last 90 days. This will be blank in the original plan, but will be completed from the first review onwards.

- Page 5 onwards: Actions in years 1, 2 and 3, organised by function (marketing, sales, finance, admin etc.). The actions in year 1 will be fairly detailed and specific, in years 2 and 3 rather less so.

Now you have your plan, but there is one more thing to do before you get motoring on the first 90 days' actions.

We strongly suggest that you put a date in the diary for the first year's half-day review sessions. They can, in fact, follow or partly replace the monthly management meeting, provided day-to-day issues do not divert attention from them. Your review sessions should be every quarter, with one informal review after 4–6 weeks to ensure the immediate tasks are being addressed and everyone is 'on the same page'.

The review sessions

The rules and process for running effective management meetings (see Chapter 4 pages 157–159) apply equally to the review sessions. The notes from the previous review are the agenda for the next one, and those responsible for preparing data and analysis should have it done and distributed to the rest of the team in good time.

The meeting conversation may jump from one topic to another. This is not a bad thing, provided every outstanding action has been discussed and either brought to a conclusion or the next step agreed. Make sure there is agreement on how to proceed in the next 90 days, with up to six specific actions and, if appropriate, the person responsible for each action decided on.

When it comes to writing up the notes afterwards, the design of the plan comes into its own. This approach will keep the minutes focused on what is important at the time and should keep them to no more than seven or eight pages:

- Save the current notes under a new file name.

- Cover page: Update the title and date and the date of the next review meeting.

- Page 1: Confirm the goal and milestones are still valid or change if necessary.

- Page 2: Add the previous quarter's revenue to the table, plus any brief comments.

- Page 3:

  ▷ Summarise the key events, successes and failures of the 90 days just gone in the first one or two paragraphs.

  ▷ Move the actions from the 90 days just gone to page 4.

  ▷ Write a sentence that sums up the focus of the next 90 days, followed by a detailed description of what actions need to be taken and, if appropriate, the person responsible for each action.

- Page 4:

  ▷ Make a comment on progress under each of the newly arrived actions and under any other actions still outstanding from previous periods. Outstanding actions may now have a string of comments from when they first appeared, which may have you asking why they have not been completed.

  ▷ Remove any item identified as complete last time.

- Page 5 and following:

  ▷ Remove any item identified as complete last time.

  ▷ Make any appropriate comment under each item. It is not necessary to repeat what has already been written, but these comments serve to ensure you keep the 90-day actions in line with the direction you originally foresaw, or to explain why they have changed or been 'put on the back burner'.

Financing your Growth

"I can do it myself!" (Matthew's daughter, aged 3½, in 1982)

It may well be possible to grow your business without financial help from outside.

Many start-ups, young businesses and, in fact, many business owners generally, are determined to launch and grow their businesses by financing it themselves and not incurring debt. Many of them succeed, because the funds they start with – wherever they come from – tide them over until the business starts generating enough income from sales to meet their financial obligations, fund whatever they need to continue growing and provide enough to live on.

However, there are times when an injection of cash is necessary to meet the expenses of growing the business before sales revenue catches up. In our experience, too many owners of young businesses try to finance their growth from sales revenue, but find they need funds in order to generate sales! This is a classic business illustration of *Catch 22* (the title of a novel by Joseph Heller, published in 1961).

You will have running costs from day one. These will not just be administrative overheads like telephones, cars, registrations and fees, but also marketing costs such as website, business cards, event fees and so on. Some start-up or 'seed' capital is therefore necessary and will often be sourced from personal funds, friends or family.

However, the owners of more established businesses will often find that serious growth is going to need serious funds and, if these are not readily to hand, they will have to address the first of two key questions.

Should I look for external funding or not?

There is some risk attached, whichever way you jump. Such is life.

Let us consider two scenarios, one with external investment, the other without.

If you do not seek external funding, what will it take to generate the growth you want? This means: how much must you sell, how and at what cost will you sell it and how long will it take?

What does your cash flow look like between now and then? To put it another way, do you have enough cash to see you through until you make the sales you need and, most importantly, until you get paid?

Now answer the same questions, but with a cash injection. Your cash flow must now allow for repayments and interest, but does the extra cash allow you to do things, and especially to generate the necessary sales revenue, that you couldn't do without it?

There is risk, of course, in taking on a debt. But it is not necessarily bad; it all depends on individual circumstances. Many people routinely have a mortgage and accept it as one of life's normal, even desirable, expenses, given the anticipation of long-term growth in the value of their property.

Perhaps, with a proper business plan that brings together all the elements necessary to run and grow the business, the risk is less with a cash injection than without it.

Let us now assume that you decide to look for a cash injection of some sort.

Where will I get it and what will I have to do to get it?

We will assume you have exhausted any sources of your own that you are prepared to put into the business, but even when you are sinking your own funds into it, you should still ask yourself the same questions as you would if someone approached you and asked "Will you invest in my business?"

With the shoe on the other foot, it is perhaps easier to understand what a potential investor (bank, private investor, relative or friend) will want to know and what conditions they are likely to impose to minimise the risk to their investment. Your understanding will go a long way to reassuring them that their money is well placed with you.

So what would you want to know if you were being asked for funds? We suggest the answer boils down to three key questions:

1. How safe is my money?
2. What return will I get?
3. When will I get paid?

A bank or other debt-based lender will answer the second two by setting out the repayment terms and interest rate, and their only concern is whether you can repay it in full. An investor is betting on the business becoming successful and may lay out a repayment schedule, expect a minimum return in a certain time frame or demand a share of the business, or some combination of these. You will have to decide if the terms are acceptable, but in order to get the offer on the table, the real question to address is the first one: **how safe is it?**

The key now is to inspire confidence. Banks, in particular, will focus their attention on the directors and on the track record of the company, with respect to 4 'S's:

Serviceability (ability to pay)

- Turnover – amount, rhythm, seasonal variation
- Net profit, adjusted for exceptional items such as depreciation, one-offs etc.
- Drawings and dividends (i.e. what historically happens to the profit)
- Projected turnover and profit and the basis for the projection
- The order book, work in progress and sales pipeline

Suitability

- Owners' strengths and weaknesses
- The key personnel
- Their stake in the business (what they have invested)
- Directors' loans and drawings versus the balance sheet
- Business organisation

Security

- Is the property owned? Is there an existing charge on it?

- Are there life policies or personal guarantees?

- Is there ring-fenced (escrow) cash in the business?

- Are there any government-backed guarantees?

Stakes

- What has been invested and by whom?

- Have other sources of funding been approached? Have they offered anything yet and, if so, on what terms (e.g. 50% match funding)?

Banks tend to take a heavily financial view of the business and place great emphasis on financial track record, as you may expect; finance is their business, after all.

Other investors and certain other lenders may take a more business-oriented view, so at this point it is useful to recall the diagram of how business is organised, reproduced here from Chapter 1, because each block of activity suggests the questions they may ask in addition to information on your track record.

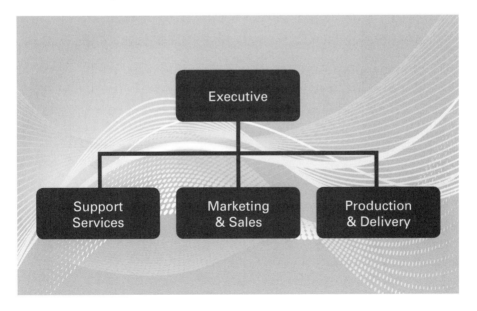

Executive/management

- What relevant qualifications and competencies do you and your management team possess?

- Are you, and they, committed to and passionate about the business?

- Do you have a clear goal for the business and a well-constructed, well-thought-out plan to achieve it?

- Do you have a clear, realistic financial plan?

- Are you clear what the investment is needed for, how it will be spent and what outcome you expect?

- How much of your own money have you invested in the business?

- What return is expected from the investment and when?

Organisation

- What systems are in place to:

  ▷ control your finances?

  ▷ manage your people?

  ▷ receive and respond to enquiries?

  ▷ ensure products and services are delivered correctly and on time?

  ▷ ensure invoices are issued and the money collected?

- How is your business protected from a serious interruption (especially to your IT systems)?

Marketing

Funding is often requested to develop and launch new products and/or enter new markets, or to expand in an established market. This may trigger questions such as:

- What research have you done that tells you there is a market for your product/service?

- What proves you have a competitive advantage in supplying it?

- How will you reach and communicate with this market?

- How will you tell which channels work and which don't?

- How will you price your product or service to maximise your return while remaining competitive?

- How will the competition react and what will your response be?

Sales

- What systems do you have to manage your prospects?

- How capable are you or your sales force in engaging with prospects and closing the deal?

- Does your product mix cover your overheads and deliver adequate profit?

- How many customers do you have and how are they distributed?

- How reliant are you on one or two key accounts?

- What is the risk and consequence of losing one of them?

Production and delivery

- Do you have the systems to ensure quality and consistency?

- Do you have the resources and organisation to deliver everything you sell?

These are examples of the questions any prudent investor will ask if you approach them for money. You may think of others, and they certainly will!

In the end, though, the better organised and thought-out your plan is, and the more you anticipate and answer their questions, the more likely it is that you will inspire their confidence and trust. It will not guarantee the result you want, but it will go a long way to giving the bank manager, lender or investor that 'nice warm feeling' that precedes the answer: yes, of course, how much do you want?

Summary

There are many ways to finance the growth of a business, and by addressing certain key basic questions, you will be in a much better position to decide on the most appropriate type of funding for your business and to prepare your business case.

When looking at serious injections of finance, we strongly recommend that you take expert advice, in order to identify alternative funding sources, to determine your investment readiness and to prepare to face potential investors.

And Finally…

A good friend of ours always finishes his speaking engagements, workshops and seminars with a final question: what is the one thing you will take from today?

If you have read through this book, you may have noticed a common thread running through it.

We suggest that if you take nothing else, you will pick up on that common thread and do the one thing that will make all the difference to the way you run your business and achieve your ambitions, and that is…**measure**, **track** and **monitor!**

- You **measure** things in order to track them.

- You **track** things in order to monitor them.

- You **monitor** things in order to be sure you are on target and to make changes if not.

For example:

- Prospects – how good your marketing is.

- Customers – how good your sales activity is.

- Customer service – how well you are satisfying your customers and getting repeat business.

- Finances – are you breaking even, making enough to live, achieving your growth target?

- Administration – are you getting your invoices out on time?

- Debtors and creditors – are you getting your money in and your suppliers paid?

- Time management – are you getting everything important done and do you still have time for the family?

- Management meetings – are they regular? Are they effective? Do they run to time?

- Goals, milestones and objectives: are you achieving them?

The MOMENTUM Programme

At the beginning, we described this book as the written version of the MOMENTUM programme.

But what if the written word is not enough or not suitable for your needs?

If this is the case, for whatever reason, it may be helpful to assess whether the MOMENTUM programme could help you move your business forward.

Let us start by recalling how the MOMENTUM programme came about.

Background

Our experience and research showed that many small-business owners were tied up in running their businesses day to day, trying to bring their products and services to market while dealing with internal matters like staffing, cash flow and the daily avalanche of emails. Such people needed help, but rejected conventional consultancy for at least one of these reasons:

- Accountability: advice had to be paid for, whether or not it was helpful or relevant or if it made a difference to the business.

- Implementation: even good advice and well-written reports often did not make things happen, especially in small businesses where a few people had to do everything.

- Cost: standard day rates soon mounted up, especially if the consultant was asked to help with the implementation as well.

These insights led to the creation of the MOMENTUM programme. Confronting each of these issues in turn, it was designed to help business owners to generate a plan for growth, to make it happen, to be affordable and, with its unique guarantee of success, to reassure them of its quality and the outcome they could expect. It provided director-level experience and expertise, as well as hands-on assistance and access to a wide network of opportunities and support.

Is it suitable for any business owner?

The answer is yes, provided the business owner embarks on it for the right reasons and with the right expectation. It will require sustained effort, so the owner needs to be serious about wanting to grow a business that has the potential to grow. The owner must be prepared to accept advice, to be held accountable for their actions and to change what may be strongly held views or much-cherished activities. Finally, there must be sufficient funds to cover the cost of the programme until the business growth kicks in. This final point emphasises that the MOMENTUM programme is not a short-term fix, but a longer-term programme for sustained growth. If immediate results are needed or there are insufficient funds, a different solution will be necessary.

These criteria also explain why MOMENTUM works best on businesses that are already established (at least 1–2 years old); the process works perfectly well with start-ups, but generally it is more difficult for an owner to be sure that the criteria can be met.

For all these reasons, we have a preliminary discussion, at no cost, to ensure that the programme is suitable for you and your business. Once we are both assured on that point and you are comfortable with the terms of the programme, we can start.

The mechanism

The MOMENTUM programme is a three-year programme for which you pay a set-up fee followed by 35 fixed monthly payments by standing order. This enables you to know exactly what you will pay, and when, with minimum administrative effort.

The programme operates in three distinct phases.

Phase 1 is a series of half-day meetings with you – normally four or five over the first month – in which we analyse every aspect of your business, following the same sequence as in the book. This identifies the business goal and the key growth areas and establishes the key objectives that determine what has to happen.

In Phase 2, we jointly develop the 'growth plan', based on an evaluation of this analysis. This becomes our commitment to each other: it is your commitment to carry out the actions agreed in the plan and our commitment to provide the help, support and advice necessary for you to stick to the plan. This phase can take one or two more meetings, depending on the complexity of the business. The plan is detailed in year 1, less so in years 2 and 3, but with specific actions for the first 90 days.

Phase 3 is the implementation phase. We meet for a half-day every quarter to assure ourselves that the original goal and objectives are still the right ones, to review the previous 90 days and to plan the next 90. During the period between the quarterly meetings, you have unlimited access to us via telephone or email, which in our clients' experience is a particularly valuable feature.

These review meetings are essential to the success of the programme as, first of all, they are the time when you take yourself out of day-to-day life to think about the business and, secondly, they are when you are held to account for what you have done (or not done!). This is perhaps the secret ingredient that makes the MOMENTUM programme really successful!

The MOMENTUM guarantee

To our knowledge, this is unique in the UK consulting world. We are so confident that the advice and assistance you receive will help you grow your business that **we guarantee** that, if you follow all our advice and implement the steps we suggest, your profits will increase over the 3-year period by **at least three times the cost of your investment**. This is our accountability to you for the end result!

If you are interested in learning more about the MOMENTUM programme and its suitability for your business, you can either contact us by phone or email, or book a review session on our website.

Notes